Everyplace I Go is Haunted

Everyplace I Go is Haunted

Richard L. Smith

ISBN (Softcover): 1-932205-85-3
Library of Congress Control Number: 2003114458

Word Association Publishers
205 5th Avenue
Tarentum, PA 15084
www.wordassociation.com

Dedication

To my sweet Mary: Thank you for letting me be myself.

Acknowledgement

For the wonderful drawings in
"Everyplace I Go Is Haunted"
Many thanks to Eve Myles, a
nationally known artist whose works
include portraits of Betty and Gerald Ford,
Elizabeth Taylor, and "*Kennedy &
Caroline*", the famous painting now
hanging in the Kennedy Museum in
Boston.

Visit Eve at her website:
www.evemyles.com
or email at :
Evezart@aol.com

Prologue

You know, I was going to put a bunch of recipes in this spot just to see if anyone would notice....Everyone had told me that no one reads the prologue in a book ! And maybe they are right. I myself am usually anxious to get started on a good book, and I always head right for chapter one, thinking I'll come back to the introductions later.

So, with that in mind, I'll just make this short and sweet in case some of you do read this, and *I strongly recommend that you do!*

This book is about my adventures with Mary in ghost hunting. And, more specifically, it's about the voice communication we experienced with those who have passed on from their lives on Earth, and who seem to be lingering in a state of existence very near the Earth plane. Mary and I can occasionally hear their voices with our own ears, and we easily talk back and forth with them by means of a recording technique using digital recorders and computers.

This is real...it is not a trick or gimmick.

Recording of these voices is, in fact, something that anyone with a serious commitment can successfully do, and these same people will usually find that opening their awareness to the spirit world will improve the development of their psychic and claireaudient abilities (as has happened with Mary and I).

We have found that the entities in the astral region allowing exchange of voice communication (EVP-electronics voice phenomena), still seem to possess the very human qualities and attitudes that they had in their Earth existence. Their personalities seem to survive death for at least the duration of their stay in that plane. We find often that comments by spirit entities exhibit human traits such as humor, love, jealousy, sarcasm and even rage. Their messages can be laced occasionally with swearing, vulgarities, references to sexuality, and some may be obnoxious, rude, or downright mean-spirited in their behavior. But fortunately, most are very pleasant, and apparently eager to communicate.

After fulfilling the purpose of this interim existence, many believe that the spirit then begins the ascent through the many spiritual levels in the journey towards oneness with God.

We hope you enjoy sharing experiences with Mary and I as we explore this "other world '' by communicating with voices from beyond the veil ....

CAUTION:

Although Mary and I have found the study of EVP to be rewarding and our efforts have resulted in comfort to us gained from the awareness of an afterlife, some negative contacts have been experienced along the way. This study may not be for the squeamish or faint of heart. It may not be for you. It is advised that all who undertake interaction with any paranormal occurances (such as EVP) should exercise sound judgement and spend as much time as possible reading, researching, and familiarizing themselves with the experiences of others who have knowledge to share in this area before trying personal contact with the spirit world.

Contents

Listening to Voices of the Dead

WHAT IS EVP?

EVP (Electronics Voice Phenomenon) is simply defined as the capture of unexplained voices on tape or digital recordings. These are sometimes heard by ear as well, but usually they are faint, halting, difficult to discern brief phrases, occasionally with odd or improper structure or grammar. Sometimes the words seem to be in a sing-song or melodic pattern.

Some voice samples may be cluttered with noise and interference, thus requiring the use of audio filters and electronics noise reduction programs. This may sometimes also result in diminished quality of the voice signal. It is not yet a precise science, and much technical work is yet to be done in this field.

These voice patterns were first discovered, seriously studied, and written about as early as the 1950's.

Since then, many researchers have been startled to find that not all EVP is a random event. Many investigators (myself included) have been called by their names, had their spoken questions answered, and even received messages from loved ones who have passed on!

Techniques for capturing EVP are varied. Extensive laboratory methods have been devised using "white noise generators" (from which the voices must be electronically extracted) and others tune to open frequency ranges on radio and TV bands as a noise source. The simplest method though, is just to open a fresh new audio tape, stick it in a good quality portable recorder with a "plug-in" microphone, (don't use built-in mikes, they're too noisy) and give it a try.

Better yet, go with a digital recorder..the more modestly priced the better. Their IC components are notoriously noisey, and are thought by some for that reason to be their own inherent source of white noise energy. Also, they are quite compatible with most home computer systems, giving one the ease of filing or storage, as well as simpler access to noise reducing programs.

EVP THEORY

There may be as many theories about EVP as there are people actually working with the phenomenon. But I'd like to comment only on two theories that seem to follow, as a general rule, a model to which I can attest as a result of my own personal observation and experience.

One theory, described simply as the "survival" theory states that there is a component of ourselves that exists also in a "mental, spiritual, or astral plane." It can exist separately from our physical body, and will survive the body death experience. Although this essentially controlling mental awareness resides within our body during our lifetime, it allows us to just step from our bodies at the moment of passing, and eventually to rejoin the true reality of our existence in the spirit world.

I have found that my EVP experiences consistently follow a typical model fashioned after the "survival" theory. This is most persuasively demonstrated by those recorded voices that make comments of a personal nature to an individual, often imparting information that should only be known by that person and the spirit entity. In many cases, answers to questions are given, and further comments seemingly in context with conversation or desired subjects of discussion in the EVP session. For instance, on most all field trips to cemeteries, at some point I will usually ask for entities who can see or hear me, to speak their names. In almost every case, at least in the larger cemeteries, I am able to record several voices speaking names that can also be seen on gravestones. We have to remember that the entity may get the impression that we can hear them as they speak, and thus misunderstand what we can and cannot do, so it is necessary when conducting EVP to make clear statements of intentions.

Another theory model which very closely follows my experience with electronic voice phenomena, may offer the skeptic some rather abstract, but nevertheless possible, explanation for the voices without accepting the "life after death" survival scenario. This theory, however, does include some acceptance of principles of psychic energy, as well as new and unproven theoretical concepts of physics, and, in particular, some aspects of theory as it may possibly apply to a " holographic universe, scalar waves, and other such theoretical quantum realities." Nevertheless, practical experience seems to fit the model, in spite of the big words. A simplified explanation follows...

We have all taken note in our studies, of various scientific observations stating that matter, or energy, cannot be destroyed. Disregarding any arguments regarding nuclear fission, or some other non related issue, most will probably agree that theoretically at least, if a sound (a form of energy) is produced in our reality, it can and should exist forever and could be located and reproduced, if and when, we have the technical means to do so.

Could it then be, that any sound (or in this case, any spoken phrase), may be "stored" in some manner in an etheric or quantum area which might be referred to as a "field," containing all sound energy, and described, defined, and categorized by the specific parameters of each sound and its unique properties? If that could be so, (and remember, we are talking "theory" here,) then we must accept that such an archive may at some point, be accessed.

If this theoretical arena of spoken phrases does exist, could it be further possible that it's information could be "tapped" by a mental or psychic inquiry from an individual whose psychic abilities are sensing said archive, and would a "psychic search" by that sensitive individual be able to access this archive looking for sounds and emotions of a particular description? In other words, if you were psychic, and promoting an aura of "loving energy," would you then be able to more easily access similar energies of the same description? Would a person emitting psychic energy of a loving, caring nature be more likely to intercept other energies and messages from beyond in a loving and caring state of emotional energy as well?

Those of you who have read my website may be familiar with the article "Columbia On My Mind." In that article, I describe my visit to the gateway of the NASA Space Center the day after the Columbia shuttle disaster. At that location, I encountered EVP messages which seemed specifically caring, grieving and consoling in nature. But, in view of the before mentioned theory, are those messages from sympathetic spirits observing myself and the group of grieving visitors?.......Or......could it be instead that all I was doing was communicating a type of "mediumship" or psychic energy, and connecting with similar energies emitted by the combined strength of emotions emanating from the grieving crowd surrounding me?

This would seem to suggest that such a theory might explain the incidence of personal observation, intuition, and psychic episodes as described by individuals. But, so far, this incidence of mediumship doesn't necessarily mean that such energies would also be transmitted to a recording device. Recorders typically just pick up sound, and transfer it by an electronic process. We are left somewhat lacking in an explanation for the actual transfer of a psychic signal to an actual voice audio that can be heard by the human ear.

The theory involving the actual transfer of voice to the recording device is a debated and controversial subject. That the EVP does in fact, show up on the recordings, and has no apparent explanation, is not the debate. It happens, therefore it is. But the transfer of signal through the many devices used for these recordings (digital and tape type recorders, computers, video cameras, television, telephones, and phone message devices, etc., are many of the devices which have been known to capture EVP, or ITC (Instrumental Trans Communication-in the case of video signals) is a matter that requires the continued research and documentation of engineers and technicians devoted to locating the direct source, or sources, for EVP. The answers will be determined by technology, and most likely will include a technology that encompasses new directions in the study of physics.

For those of you who would require a bit more technical explanation, let me point out that certain aspects of the recording process (as it applies to our simple recordings of EVP in the field) are not all that complicated and there is perhaps one issue that still needs to be addressed here. And that would be the matter of how a device that is designed to record a human "voice" can wind up with a voice recorded on that device "without us being able to hear it also?"

One of the first pieces of equipment a paranormal investigator will acquire is a "magnetic field detector" or field measuring device. In almost all documentable paranormal events, it has been found that aberrations in magnetic fields will occur. In some cases, fields will appear where there were none, and in concert with certain other anomalous phenomena, such as notable variations of temperature. This magnetic field issue may turn out to be an important key to the unwinding of the EVP mystery, and here's one of the clues that lead us in that direction........

Essentially, the recorder is a device that uses a magnetic field in the early stages of electronic circuitry, thus creating the suspicion that magnetic field changes may be indicative of a direct influence on the recording device. A microphone, for instance, (as it is normally found on a typical inexpensive recorder that you and I may use), is a fairly simple and uncomplicated device. It uses an internal mechanism, such as a diaphragm or carbon particles, constructed in such a way as to be sensitive to the waves generated by sound. These waves create a reaction within the device which is further transduced to a magnetic signal proportional in various parameters to the sound waves received. Then the newly created electronic signal is selectively processed, amplified by specific circuitry, and delivered to another magnetic device such as the heads of a recorder, which transmit again another field effecting the transfer of a magnetically arranged pattern on the tape. A digital recorder uses a different process at this point, but in both cases, the unprotected circuits are susceptible to any number of influences of magnetic field aberration at many points within the electronic processing of the signal.

The bottom line is that the recorder can be quite vulnerable to magnetic field influence, and this may actually contribute to the possiblility of recording on the device without even using a microphone. All that might be needed is the insertion of the appropriate field "after" the mike. Now, that would seem to indicate that "spirits" may be using some sort of technology themselves. Don't laugh that one off.......some of the most highly respected research and scientific documentation ever done in EVP indicates exactly that premise! In our next chapter on "History of EVP" be sure and do some extra reading on the researchers mentioned there for information on the more technical aspects of EVP analysis.

THE HUMAN FACTOR
the final obstacle

After having covered a few of the basic electronic, environmental, and procedural problems that may be encountered in the collection and processing of EVP, finally we are faced with a more fundamental area of potential difficulty.....that of the considerable variation of human abilities, personalities, preferences, predispositions, talents (or lack thereof), prejudices, and just plain stubbornness that you will encounter in the study of EVP.

One of the more common things we immediately notice, is the tendency of people to interpret the wording of an EVP message in slightly, and occasionally, radically different ways.

In the case of the "slight" differences noted, there are more acceptable explanations than we have available time and space for elaboration. But, consider just a few of the more obvious:

1. Differences in the human hearing ability, involving age, physical health, etc.

2. Conditions under which any person may hear any particular EVP sample (some people may not consider external influences of noise level and distractions, etc., and further, they may not utilize an acceptable audio system for proper reproduction of specific frequencies in any given EVP sample.

3. One of the most commonly unnoticed prejudices shown by people may be as a result of dialect and accent influences. People have been known to misunderstand speech because of extremely subtle and minor differences, including the speed at which words are spoken. In fact, you might be surprised at how much an individual relies on visual reference and body language, etc. as a part of the process of verbal communication. Also, our minds can be well ahead of our ears as we communicate with others, as we depend on context of the subject to anticipate what may be coming in a conversation, whereas EVP messages come to us without mental preparation for subject and context.

4. In some rare circumstances, for whatever reason shall remain unknown to us all, certain individuals simply will not hear EVP no matter what efforts are made by others to assist them. This may occur in spite of the fact that an entire roomful of people, in the presence of this single negative individual, can be in complete agreement about each and every aspect of a selection of EVP audio, to the exclusion of the sole unique nonparticipant.This seems to be nothing more, or less, than a psychological refusal on the part of the individual, and not necessarily a result of any physical reason. As an analogy, one could surmise that even if coached by the greatest basketball coach or player known to the world, a person who steadfastly states that they can not put a basketball through the hoop will indeed be most unlikely to accomplish the feat, in spite of the efforts of the experts. This person is simply not ready for the experience.....maybe some other time. And I would like to further caution against the advisability of inviting such a negative personality along on a project with the expectation of collecting EVP. There is no doubt that certain individuals can influence negatively any psychic phenomenon involving the possibility of mediumship in such a manner as is associated with the relationship between EVP and its collectors and experimenters.

5. In the case of persons hearing radically different interpretations of the same EVP, it can be the sum of more than one of previously mentioned issues, or it can be that there actually is more than one EVP message on the same recording. The multiple voice EVP is, in fact, a most common occurance, and considered a matter for the more advanced EVP investigator,as it usually requires the use of some advanced form of audio filtering or electronic or digital processing to produce a sensible message from the jumble of several. Unprocessed multiple EVP may sometimes sound like a recording made in a crowded room, in which one is straining to hear the message from a single individual.

IMPORTANT:
It takes some time to develop a skilled ear for listening to the many subtle variances of EVP audio. It is an acquired skill, and comes eventually to all who work with EVP, and likewise is noticed by all as quite absent in the beginner. This can indeed be frustrating at first, but experience provides the solution.

A WARNING:
Most all who take the study of EVP seriously, will, after a period of time, begin to become aware of an increase in claireaudient abilities as a result of communicating and attracting the interest of the spirit world. In other words, there will be a time when you are hearing, under certain circumstances, the voices of spirits without the use of technical means. Be advised that the undertaking of EVP study can change your world forever.....

The study of EVP produces an interesting mix of metaphysics and physical science. This we can readily accept, but unfortunately mainstream scientists may not be so agreeable.

To further confuse the issue, EVP study and experiments have indicated the likelihood that static or background noise, such as "white noise" from a sound generator or noise from tuning between radio or communication bands, is used as raw material by which the EVP process (by entity or mediumship) forms words into messages with meaning and context.. Many successful EVP experimenters will play a white noise source in the background while conducting EVP recording sessions. This is not mandatory for EVP collection, but evidence seems to indicate that more detailed messages can be received in this manner.

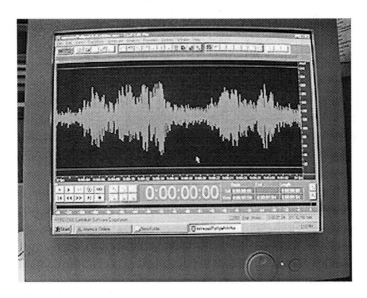

This computer monitor in Rich's lab shows the waveform of an actual digital signal from an EVP recording captured during a visit to a cemetery in Austin, Texas. The waveform shown is being electronically filtered and amplified to clarify the voice signal.

A question regarding understanding or interpreting EVP email:

Hi Rich,

Was just on your internet website. Excellent! I have a question: On your website article " Hospital Spirits ghosts and EVP," I just want to know if you hear the same thing I do on that clip relating to the boisterous spirit exclamation (green tie). I hear him say " I amGod." The clips are so clear. I could play on this site all day. Thanks,

Karen. (AAEVP)

reply from Rich:

Hi Karen;

Thanks for stopping by the website... and thanks for the interesting comments. I have not heard those particular words from that EVP..... However, I have had several comments on that very one, including several who have heard the same words you heard. I frequently find that there are more than one message on EVP recordings (some superimposed on top of others), and it seems to me that the narrow band frequency filtering from digital processors like Cool Edit, may be responsible for an easy shift to another embedded message when the EVP is replayed on another sound system with different specs than the one that did all the original processing.

As a comparison, I'm sure you have noticed when listening to radio music, that the "bass" response is noticeably missing on inferior music systems and AM radio. But when the same source is run through a sound system with different frequency response specs, you could hear the bass response and much more than you did on the other. A similar thing can occur when we simply change sound replay systems while listening to an EVP that has been seriously modified in frequency composition. Indeed, in the case of this specific EVP selection, you are not the first who has heard that exact interpretation. It is likely that I could take that particular sample, rerun it again through Cool Edit, and locate the exact voice which you described....giving us not one, but two messages recorded at the same time......only one of which would be more easily heard on any particular sound system or with any particular set of ears. hope this has been some help.........Rich

ELECTRONICS VOICE PHENOMENA
HEAR ACTUAL VOICES FROM BEYOND
On your "Every Place I go is Haunted" CD

READ BEFORE LISTENING TO YOUR EVP SELECTIONS

Although it is possible to get EVP with fairly common, inexpensive recording apparatus, usually only "Class A" voice signals are captured by the beginner. (Class A are the strongest and clearest). Paranormal Investigations of Texas currently uses equipment and analysis technique which would be considered laboratory level quality and thus is able to achieve success levels which should not be expected by the beginner.

Paranormal Investigations of Texas uses a digital process of "cleaning" the recordings which, through the use of electronic filters and clippers, reduces or removes various noise and interference levels. We also have the capability to increase gain and amplify very weak signals which may not be easily heard with the human ear. In addition, we have found that there often can be more than just one voice to be found in an EVP sample, and when we remove the lesser of the amplitudes, we usually wind up with a voice signal that is very narrow in composition.

This makes it imperative that the listener use only a good, CD music quality sound system when listening to the EVP selections on your EVP disk. A quiet, studious atmosphere is strongly recommended, and the use of good quality headsets may be a plus. Some of these samples have been engineered to a very narrow frequency range, and if an inferior computer sound card is used or a small or inferior speaker system, the entire voice signal may not be reproduced or an entirely different frequency range signal may partially appear.

Remember, EVP listening is an acquired ability. Your ear will get better at hearing and translating as you work more and more with EVP. In fact, a large percentage of those who study EVP have reported an increase in development of clairaudient abilities. You'll get back out of it what you put into it!

A Brief History Of EVP

EVP is not an established science. If I were a nuclear physicist, I suppose I would be expected to discuss all matters of fission and nuclear energy with detail and authority. But are there actually top level scientists at institutions of higher learning involved in the study of EVP phenomena? And if so, can they speak authoritatively to the dedication and documentation of years of detailed and structured study on this fascinating, but little known, hard evidence of communication with the beyond?

Most folks are amazed to find, when exposed to the reality of electronics voice phenomena, that there is a lengthy history of decades of documented study on the subject, including acceptance of EVP by none other than the Catholic Church. We will take a closer look at that history later in this chapter.

Mainstream science is known for being slow to accept new concepts. Of course, absolute proof is the backbone of science, so it is understandably difficult for researchers to undertake new theory, and set out to prove something that flys in the face of accepted study. Also, there is the problem of motivation and budgeting. Scientists have to make a living too, and it's understandable that a scientist may want only the most credible studies listed on their resume when applying for positions in high level institutional, governmental, and industrial research.

Scientific EVP study has perhaps taken a back seat to more pressing issues of daily needs in our society. But what then of our spiritual needs? What could be more valuable to a person than to be given special knowledge of the fact that the soul survives, in an extraordinarily conscious manner, after passing from life on this earth? Again, it's perhaps understandable that scientists would rather leave that part to churches and other spiritual areas of study.

So, we find ourselves making progress in small steps, pretty much without (so far) any huge support from the scientific community.

The wonderful thing about human nature, however, is that our adventuresome and curious minds will not stand for ignoring such an obvious and documentable phenomenon. And that attitude extends to an occasional educated and gifted scientific mind whose priorities are not etched in the stone faced skepticism and indifference of rank and file science. Thank goodness for such mavericks in the scientific community. Indeed, notable work, albeit it on the sidelines and somewhat out of sight, is being done on the study of EVP and the spiritual realm that includes such novel experiences as electronics voice phenomena.

Regarding any debate that may come up as to the issue of authenticating EVP; actually that part of the issue is pretty much beyond debate. Actual EVP is considerably easier to acquire than "faking or hoaxing" such complex audio, and a hoax would, of course, be detected by analysis. The real topic of debate is more or less on the true origin or source of such mysterious voices. And the extensive history of investigating that mysterious origin of electronics voice phenomena is quite surprising.

As a matter of fact, at the beginning of the last century, Thomas Edison, Marconi, and Nikola Tesla, inventors and genius innovators of electricity and electronics communication, spent many of their last years trying desperately to prove their own theories which implied that communication with other dimensions and spiritual planes would be possible through technology.

Documentation of EVP study began in earnest in the mid 20th century, and it soon became clear that the issue was not of proving the existence of actual EVP (thousands upon thousands of voices of unknown source were quickly accumulated), but the burden of explaining its source within the parameters of physics known at the time would be the chore of all who endeavored to solve the mystery.

In 1959, Russian born Sir Friedrich Jurgenson, an artist and film producer, recorded his deceased mothers voice on a reel to reel recorder while at his estate in Sweden. He went on to record thousands of discarnate voices and is usually regarded as the "father of EVP." Dr Hans Bender, heading a team of researchers at the University of Freiburg, Germany, made a thorough study of Jurgenson's tapes, even using voice print analysis, and concluded the voices had an unknown paranormal source.

By 1965, a well known Latvian psychologist, a graduate of Edinburgh University and author of six books, Dr Konstantin Raudive, had developed an intense interest in physical forms of mediumship. After meeting Jurgenson, he set up his own research facility in Germany, and enlisted the assistance of Friedebert Karger, research physicist at the Max Planck Institute in Munich. With the addition of engineers to his staff, he was successful in eventually recording more than 100,000 discarnate voices. In 1968, Raudive published his first book on the subject of the voice phenomenon "The Inaudible Becomes Audible." Amazingly, Konstantin Raudive told his associates that he would continue his EVP studies after his death, and his voice was indeed subsequently recorded and identified by those associates after his death!

In 1982, an American, George Meek, enlisted the aid of several engineers and developed a device called "spiricom" which facilitated a two way communication with the dead. His results were published, and later, engineer Hans-Otto Koenig transmitted through Luxembourg radio a live broadcast of a two way conversation with a deceased person.

THE VATICAN AND EVP

The Catholic Church has for decades studied the EVP phenomenon, going so far as to officially sanction and approve of EVP studies with edicts issued by two popes.... Pope Paul VI, and Pope Pius XII.

In 1969, Pope Paul VI awarded Friederich Jurgenson with the "Knight Commander of the Order of St. Gregory," for his work on EVP. Jurgensen wrote, in a letter to an associate researcher of EVP....." I have found a sympathetic ear for the voice phenomenon in the Vatican. I have won many wonderful friends among the leading figures in the Holy City."

In 1990, Pope Pius XII in Rome personally corresponded with two early investigators of EVP, Italian priests Father Ernetti, and Father Gemelli.

The two priests accidentally came upon EVP while recording Gregorian chants in !952. Father Gemelli heard his own fathers voice on the tape, using a childhood nickname "Zucchini." The message stated.... "Zucchini, it is clear, don't you know it is I?"

The two priests, bothered by possible church conflict regarding contact with the dead, brought up the issue in a visit with Pope Pius XII in Rome.....

From Pope Pius XII:

"Dear Father Gemelli, you really need not worry about this. The existence of this voice is strictly a scientific fact and has nothing to do with spiritism. The recorder is totally objective. It receives and records only sound waves from wherever they come. This experiment may perhaps become the cornerstone for a building for scientific studies which will strengthen people's faith in a hereafter..." (Italian Journal ASTRA, June 1990, quoted Kubis and Macy, 1995:102).

Pope Pius' cousin, Rev Dr. Gebhard Frei, co-founder of the Jung Institute, was a well known psychologist who worked closely with Konstantin Raudive, and President of the International Society for Catholic Parapsychologists. He states... "All that I have read and heard forces me to believe that the voices come from transcendental, individual entities. Whether it suits me or not, I have no right to doubt the reality of the voices" (Kubris and Macy, 1995:104)

The Vatican further gave permission for its own priests to conduct their own research into the voices. Father Leo Schmid, a Swiss theologian, collected over 10,000 EVP samples, and his book "When the Dead Speak" was published in 1976.

The Yardarms Down!

"Requesting permission to come aboard, sir."

"The yardarm's Down!"

As Rich and Mary headed up the ramp to the deck of the USS Stewart, Rich was busily explaining that they were going to board the ship in the exact manner as a sailor if he were reporting for duty.. Mary and he were, of course, decked out with camera and multiple digital recorders, and anxious to find if there were any spirits lurking in the compartments or around the decks of the historical war craft from WWII.

"OK... now when we get to the top," Rich stated authoritatively," we will find a small area just inside the railing where the sailor comes to attention, and turns to salute the colors. Next, he turns to the podium behind which the Officer of the Deck will be standing, and the sailor salutes the OOD, asks for "permission to come aboard, sir." And finally, the OOD returns the salute and replies with "permission granted."

"Now, what we want to do here is to see if, by following this protocol, any spirits will notice our behavior and speak out to us. It's very likely that none of the tourists that come here will ever do anything like that. Maybe a former crewman might, but that would get the spirits attention too !"

"You ready, Mary ?"

"I guess. But I'm not sure I remember what I'm supposed to say." replied Mary

"Let's try it" said Rich. *"Now just pretend we are at the top of the gangplank, and we are going to salute the flag. That's the easy part, then what do you say to the Duty Officer?"*

"Ummm, OK, ah, so now I turn to the officer and.....but there's nobody there..." protested Mary.

"We're just pretending! Come on ..."

"Jeez...(clearing her throat)......requesting commission to board ...ummm.....that doesn't sound right..." she sputtered.

Rich repeated... "requesting permission to come aboard, sir." Okay?....

"Got it." ......and with that, they briskly headed up the ramp, and on to the walkway where the Officer of the Deck would have stood to monitor all proceedings. Rich and Mary both came to attention, and prepared to salute the colors. Turning towards the mast towering above the bridge, they searched for the flag which would be flying from the yardarm.

Oh, oh. Big problem....all the carefully laid plans for their grand entrance came to a sudden halt as they realized....there was no flag.

And, at that very moment, unknown to Rich and Mary, but solidly recorded on digital recorder, the voice of a lone sailor boomed across the otherwise silent deck......

001- "Yardarm's down!" *pronounced the sailor!!*

And with that extraordinary exclamation, a two hour haunted adventure began in earnest, as Mary and I explored the decks, fore, aft, and below, of the USS Stewart. After touring the USS Stewart, we would then head over to the dry dock immediately adjacent and visit the USS Cavalla, a WWll submarine. Before turning off our recording devices, over fifty amazing ghost voices, shouts, whispers and exclamations would be catalogued, along with a myraid of unusual bangs, clanging noises, opening and closing hatch noises and spooky squeaks. All this in spite of the fact that Mary and I were the first visitors at the pier that peaceful and quiet Monday morning. During our visit,we had the run of the ships, without an audible sound to be heard other than our footsteps and the squeal of the sea gulls circling the top deck.

(above) Here Rich stands at the helm in the flying bridge of the USS Stewart.

As memories momentarily streamed through his mind, Rich was glad he grabbed his original Navy flight jacket on this cool morning.

Rich is no stranger to the Navy. He volunteered for service with the Navy during the Vietnam war in the 60's, and the visit today to the Cavalla will be even more poignant as Rich's dad served aboard two US submarines during WWll; the USS Stickleback, and the USS Redfin. The Redfin patrolled waters near the duty asssignments of the USS Cavalla, and his dad had mentioned to Rich that Fremantle, Austrailia, was a port for the Redfin, (as was the Cavalla in the years circa 1943-46.) Perhaps these great ships had passed in the night, or maybe even the crews had liberty in the Fremantle port at the same time. Could Rich's dad have known one of the crew of the Cavalla? We shall never know, as Rich's dad and most of these brave souls have passed on...

After shooting a few photos on the bridge of the USS Stewart and a couple of the big gun mounts, we made our way down the steep ladders into the passageways of the lower decks. Along the way, we sadly took note of the obvious dis-repair of the old, proud vessel. The years of tourists crawling all over the ship, and the lack of a generous budget for maintenance had taken it's toll. Signs of the relentless onslaught of the coastal salt air were obvious, as rust and much needed paint and surface treatment were long overdue. Inside, evidence of vandalism and theft of parts of the ship for souvenirs seemed to cast a shadow over the decks of this once gallant and seaworthy vessel.

First stop was the galley, where meals were prepared for the crew. A huge cast iron grill and oven took up one whole bulkhead (wall) and along another were three huge steam operated cooking vats. Most ships of this size will have several food preparation areas, some used only for Officers and staff. We only saw this one as not all of the ship was open to visitors.

As we later discovered, virtually everywhere we went on both ships, we were being watched and followed by ghostly spirits who constantly commented on our activities and banged and clanged around doing their best to make themselves known to us. I can say they definitely succeded...... This turned out to be one of the most " spiritually active locations ever visited by Mary and myself..."

While pondering the waist-high large cooking vats, and the monstrous grill, we mentally tried to picture the busy preparations that went on in order to keep up with the needs of the crew. A moment later we filed out the exit and back into the passageway, and from out of nowhere a ghostly voice simply stated...

002- *"burned hamburger"*

It hadn't occured to us that hamburgers were a regular on the menu of a WWll destroyer escort, but when spirits speak, Mary and I just listen.....We may not always really know what is meant by some of their comments, but usually their spoken phrases are in context with the subject at hand.

Just a few steps down the passageway, we came across one of the crews heads. (For you landlubbers, a "head" is the bathroom, or toilet) Each of several compartments contained certain of the necessary elements....one had just three toilets, and a sink....another had only three sinks and on the other side three showers.. Yet another had only a urinal and a toilet. At this opportune moment, a female voice clearly pounded through and onto our recordings, demanding to know.

003- _"where's the lifers?"_

Now, this was indeed most peculiar, as it is a certainty that in those days there were no females present as crew on these old warships. So, we must surmise that we were perhaps accompanied by some "tourist type ghosts," who may have had a few observations and questions of their own!

Oh...and lest we forget, for the landlubbers once more....a "lifer" is a common Navy term used to describe the old hands on the ships who made a career of the Naval service and were most usually the holders of higher rating in the Navy.

Heading down the passageway in search of new photo sites, an unusual occurance, well known to all paranormal investigators, suddenly brought a halt to the progression.

"Battery Drain!"... An instantaneous absense of battery power in a camera (or other electronics device), coinciding with intense paranormal activity and without apparent technical explanation.

The digital camera in question had fresh recharged batteries installed immediately prior to arrival at this site, and this was an unusual happenstance.This camera is capable of taking upwards of 60 or 70 photos without recharging, and probably less than 15 or 20 had been attempted at this point Nevertheless, since the batteries in the voice recorders seemed to be operating just fine, I would just have to give the benefit of the doubt at the moment, and I quickly installed a fresh set of batteries in the camera and continued after the brief interruption.

Momentarily, Mary came up with another of her rare and "startling" clairaudient revelations, as she put her arm on my shoulder and said... "Listen...did you hear that?.....he says he doesn't want us to take pictures....he's ashamed of the way the ship looks.."

Well now, things were beginning to make a little more sense with that possible explanation for the camera difficulty. As it would later turn out, even more evidence of spiritual "tampering" came up in the processing of this section of photos when several of them came out blurred or completely black apparently as the batteries failed. And, as yet unknown to us, this phenomenon would later repeat with even more intensity and spiritual demonstration on the Cavalla.

For the moment, due to the fact that two of three sets of camera batteries were in usage or drained, our ghost detective instincts prodded us onward to the USS Cavalla, the WWII submarine drydocked adjacent to the USS Stewart.

As we moved on towards the gangplank, Mary wondered out loud... "I wonder if the spirits are talking to us on the recorder? And at that moment a recorded ghost voice replied..."

004- *"Energy will get them out..."*

As is usually the case in recording ghost voices, many spirits will jump in towards the very end of a recording segment. It would seem that the spirits may be aware of the impending conclusion of their opportunity to speak and hence they quickly make their statement. In this case, a voice came through with our final communication from the USS Stewart with a message about a sailor named Frank.

Reading up on the history of the USS Stewart, we found the ship was used for the training of Navy personnel, and responsible for the wartime preparation of hundreds of sailors. Apparently, a sailor named Frank was well known among the crew, and for reasons unknown, his name was clearly heard on three other occasions during recording sessions on the USS Stewart. In all but one of those messages, all that could be understood was his name....but in the following message, the meaning was loud and clear...

005- Frank, he jumped the ship !.....

NEXT, the USS Cavalla ....The Spirits began to take control.......!

Down The Hatch

Uss Cavalla, WWll submarine in drydock Galveston Harbor

During World War ll, the Cavalla was known as the luckiest submarine in the Fleet. Even today, she is referred to as "The Lucky Lady." This submarine is one of only a handful of US subs that still exist from World War ll.

The Cavalla was launched on November 14, 1943, and during her maiden voyage and first patrol, she sank the Japanese carrier Shokaku, which had participated in the attack on Pearl Harbor and the Battle of The Coral Sea.

As an increasing menace to enemy shipping, the Cavalla completed three patrols, and also sank two freighters and a destroyer. For these successes, she was awarded the Presidential Unit Citation.

Down the hatch....main entrance from the foreward part of the sub deck

As Mary and I approached the gallant sub with anticipation, it was obvious the condition of the ship was better than the previously visited destroyer escort. Perhaps the spirits here would be in a good mood...but then again....maybe not. (As it turned out, this would certainly be a prophetic thought.)

It was still fairly early in the morning, as tourists hours go, and there was only a single couple browsing their way around the sub. We allowed them to go on well ahead of us, so as to not worry about the possibility of voice interference, noise, or otherwise. The couple dissapeared through the ship, and Mary and I were enveloped in solitude as we began our search for haunting activity.

After entering the tiny hatch and descending the steep ladder into the bowels of the sub, we found ourselves standing in the foreward torpedo room. As we would soon learn, every tiny bit of space on a submarine is used to the maximum extent, and everywhere we looked, there was nary a square inch not cluttered with dials, pipes, knobs, guages, buttons, compartments, hoses and machinery of every kind and description. This ship was indeed an engineering marvel.

Mary's spiritual "admiration society" arrives.....

Having not yet been in the sub long enough to even get our bearings, the EVP phenomena began in earnest with the appearance of a somewhat familiar subject of spirit voices for Mary...flirtation and even possesive behavior began to manifest...(and what would one expect from a crew of astral-bound sailors?) The first EVP presence seemed to indicate quite an unmistakable male tone;

006- "Mary...hot...kiss?" Then from that point it would seem that yet another sailor preferred that he be the only one allowed to express himself

007- "Jealous !" came the retort, and the spiritual clamour did nothing but increase as time went on.

Yet another sailor spoke, with possible additional indication of respect as he stated.

008- "Angel...no offense"

(Later, in the computer lab while processing the collected EVP from the sub, it was noted that there was a constant background of clanging and banging noises. This, in spite of the fact that Mary and I did not hear these banging noises while on the ship...and some of them were quite loud and startling on the recordings and would certainly have been noticable in the relatively quiet atmosphere of the sub. There was a compressor, or something like that which made a rather startling noise while we were amidships below, but this sole distraction was of course noticable to us in the deceptively peaceful atmosphere, and only served to distinguish the difference between the spooky haunted noises on the recordings and the normal sounds of below decks.)

As we continued through the ship, we passed the small officers berthing area, then one for the chief petty officers, and next we came to the captain's quarters. A most unusual EVP phenomenon occured at this point, involving the manifestation of a ghostly voice which precedes and even anticipates a human voice. In this case, not only did the ghost voice anticipate my own voice as I spoke "Officer's Quarters," but the spirit preceded my statement with "quarter deck," and then proceeded to speak the very phrase that I was about to say, and in perfect unison with my voice even as the words were spoken! Listen very carefully, and you will hear the spirit say "quarter deck" as I come into that area just outside the officer's quarters....then you will hear the spirit and myself both speak the word "officer's", and then the spirit voice tapers off as I speak "Quarters."

009- "quarter deck" (spirit voice)... "Officers quarters" (Rich)

After passing through the quarter deck, we passed the tiny ships galley and the mess hall. The mess contains four tables and looked to be the most spacious and roomy area in the entire ship. It would clearly be a gathering place for the sailors during leisure times on board, (if in fact there was such a thing!)

We then proceeded through and into a large instrument room with a passageway located to the port (left) side. At that moment, we paused for a couple of pictures, the camera once again began another battery drain! We were only able to capture two blurred images as the camera slipped into malfunction, and those two photos, although impaired by the battery drain, revealed a dark, human shape standing in the hatch at the end of the passageway!

Blurred photos are not exactly our idea of "conclusive" evidence of a ghost. However, in view of the corroborating paranormal activity here, it certainly is a very suspicious thing that this dark figure would appear at the exact moment as the second camera battery drain, and with the accompaniment of extraordinary clairaudient and documented EVP phenomena as well!

Grabbing the last set of spare charged batteries, I installed them in the camera and pondered the precarious camera situation. One more such episode and all the ghosts in the neighborhood could parade around this submarine, but there would be no camera to capture them!

Things certainly seemed to be heating up a bit. We quickly navigated the narrow instrument laden passageway, and approached the hatch, which only seconds before, had contained a dark figure. As they leaned over and stepped through into the fairly large compartment, they could see that this was the largest of the crew bunking areas. This crews quarters looked to contain as many as 30 or more bunks very tightly and closely arranged inbetween the ever present pipes, guages, buttons, knobs and so forth. Here, we took a quiet breather as Mary sat on one of the bunks. Through the silence, on the digital recording devices, came the sound of footsteps, puncuated by a heavily breathing whispering voice which exclaimed "hold me," followed by more footsteps and another dim voice saying "hugs." Ending with more noise and steps, this approximately seven second EVP demonstrates some of the noisy activity that seemed to accompany the voices on many recordings.

010- "Footsteps...(whisper).hold me...more steps.."

The previous footsteps were quite docile in comparison to the next angry, crashing, bang that rings out as Mary reads a sign in the next compartment that says

011- "Main Engine no. 1 BANG !! BANG !!"

Was it something that Mary said?   Was it the sign? The translation of this vocalization and tirade by the spirit that follows the banging is not clear. We have decided to let your imagination run with this one ! What do you think these disturbed ghosts are trying to say after the attempt to startle us with the noise?

We heard two distinctively different voices in this one......

012- "Creaking noise .... 'sugar'...sigh.."

For a while, miscellaneous voices seemed to come from everywhere with many different subjects, names and sounds, and then a familiar name re-appeared. Remember Frank, who jumped ship from the USS Stewart next door? Well now, his name appears again after another series of clangs and metallic banging sounds....sort of a loud, but concise whisper. I suppose it could be a different Frank, after all it's a common name. But a popular one today for sure!

014- "Bang...Bang ..Bang...Frank"

While immersed in deep thought about the many ghosts that express themselves around these ships, and this submarine in particular, one has to consider that the Cavalla was certainly the exception to the rule. During the second World War fifty two submarines did not make it home, taking over 3600 men down with them. One wonders if the spirits of those lost men seek the environment of the subs that did make it......maybe that helps to explain the extremely volatile and haunting scene in this ship.

At these very controls, brave men stood while making life and death decisions in the execution of 90,000 miles of travel, and 570 dives, while surviving numerous depth charge and air attacks and sinking over 34,180 tons of enemy ships..

While contemplating those lost men and a spiritual and possibly compelling attraction to such a gallant surviving sub as the Cavalla, could it stand as a beacon for passing lost sailors? ....

015- "yeah....Beacon...I am here !...."

As we proceeded towards the aft torpedo room and the ladder to the topside deck, the voices continued, and in fact, increased in such numbers per segment of recording, that many voice samples collected were later discarded for minor problems of clarity or just any technical issue that might result in extra time for processing.

During the processing of the ships' EVP recordings, it is estimated that only half the messages were retrieved and studied.. The total number of messages was probably in excess of 100 or more, and in the coming weeks several of the clearest samples were saved for this article.

At the end point in the writing of the article, I was feeling overwhelmed by the sheer numbers of voice samples,and fearing that my readers may grow weary of the topic, began to search for an end to this adventure.

Mary suggested that I go to the spirits for a solution..........and as usual....it worked.

016- "HELL BRO......THAT'LL DO !" was the reply.......

"Why hell yes," says myself, "that oughta do it !"

But, I Digress.....

Indeed, to digress and seek mental shelter for periods of contemplation can be therapeutic for the paranormal investigator....

In fact, it is often that after an intense encounter with the paranormal, such as the experiences on the USS Stewart and Cavalla, I find a need to get into myself for a bit to consider just what all this means. You know, like maybe plopping myself down (with a hot cup of green tea) on our sun deck facing the woods behind our house at an early, peaceful, hour of the morning. Or maybe a long walk in solitude on the beach.......or, if we lived a little closer to the west Texas hill country, perching on a rock overlooking a canyon and taking in a sunrise or sunset. That kind of solitude and peaceful commune with nature does wonders for the mind that has become cluttered with confusing knowledge of the spiritual existence far beyond our our own self centered corner of earth bound reality.

During these moments, I always go thru the same old consternation over the fact that all this blatant and well documented communication with the astral plane does in fact exist, and thousands of capable, knowledgeable, serious minded, sane individuals are experiencing it, and yet the general public seems to not be paying attention.

Yes, it's a fact that more studious and scientifically oriented work is being done on Electronics Voice Phenomena.. But, it's not in the public eye, and may not be for some time.

Why isn't it featured occasionally on the 6 o'clock news?...20-20.... or 60 minutes? Of course, for me it is a fact of life, and has in fact severely changed my beliefs about everything that is, and will ever be on this earth or in the universe. But then, I am directly involved...with a front row seat, so to speak.

It is likely that the average person cannot be expected to accept the notion of EVP without a really good orientation ...kind of like you will get from this book. Actually, television would be a wonderful medium with which to educate the public on EVP. Unfortunately, however, the powerful purveyors of marketing and mass media stop this process dead in its tracks. The EVP subject is very complex, and the marketers like a simple formula.

The time proven formula of fear is certainly one of the favorites of film marketers and TV producers.. They have their own ideas of what the paranormal is, and if you disagree, whether it is about truth or not, then they have no use for you. Myself, I have little use for *them*. For instance, around Halloween each year, I get numerous invitations to go on TV and radio for interviews. I turn them all down. Every one. The reason is obvious.....all they really want is a cute little gag to impress the children and give the adults a chuckle. There is rarely a true open minded forum to discuss this type of paranormal phenomena.

And of course, another large group of people is always easily controlled by the use of ridicule, another useful marketing ploy. If we were to portray paranormal as "funny," or "unbelievable," then the tongue in cheek treatment becomes the only possible outlet for expression.... This is because people are afraid to make fools of themselves by speaking out and daring to question the status quo and accepted order of things. So it's easier for them to just join the skeptical ranks of a fraternity of fools who will blind and deafen themselves in order to maintain their smug demeaner, and not take a chance on looking foolish.

And I also have to wonder if this subject might appear to be just a little too complex in some ways to attract the average person's interest. You would be surprised how difficult it is just to engage any random individual in conversation about this subject. For instance, in interviews with just "average folks," I have personally found three distinct issues which get in the way of allowing involvement with communicating with spirits from beyond.

1. *Technical aspects* - people who are not knowledgeable of electronics, and the technical aspects of processing EVP, are somewhat reluctant to trust the information provided by sources which they may not totally comprehend. That's understandable, but when people DO get involved with EVP, they usually find that this area is not so complicated as they had once thought...

2. *Fear*.....yep, it's just fear of the unknown, pure and simple. For sure, not all folks are direct in their statement about this area of concern, but this fearful reluctance is quite obvious to me. A secondary and powerfully deep seated aspect of this fear, comes from a sudden awareness of having to face the fact that one's life may not have thus far proceeded in a completely moral, organized, and proper manner. Here, the person can exhibit panic at the thought that EVP is bringing them face to face with the actual existence of spirits from an after death dimension. And this extraordinarily powerful revelation, along with that fearful realization that they have not been living their lives in a productive manner, causes them to head for the door, and fast....Yep...I've seen it, and in fact, I've been there myself, you betcha!

3. *religion*-The basics as compiled by psychics, studies by paranormal researchers and investigators, and out-of-body and near death experiencers, etc., point to a spiritual realm of existence to which we return after our life on earth. It does appear that the voices captured by EVP may in fact be actual brief messages from spirits in those dimensional areas. If so, then many folks who hold rigid views of religious doctrine may not care to approach or even discuss the subject. This is indeed unfortunate, as my own opinion is that the serious study of EVP can enhance and further strengthen one's convictions of religious principle and value to society.

Well, for this particular moment of contemplative therapy, instead of the sun deck (it's raining) I've taken my two cups of hot green tea, with honey, to the computer and recorded a couple of my thoughts for sharing with my book readers. In fact, I think I am now refreshed and ready for a new adventure.....I wonder what will come up next?!

The Whispering Cowboy

In the winter of 2001, Mary and I finally got around to visiting the local Alta Loma Cemetery. The cemetery is actually very close to our neighborhood, and we had not realized that the cemetery was so old, or we probably wouldn't have waited so long to get over there.

The city has grown around the burial grounds now, and being surrounded by homes, we were wondering if local folks in this small town might not take well to a couple of strangers wandering around their cemetery with cameras, electronics measuring devices, and recording apparatus. We decided we would make our first visit a brief one.

The weather was nice, the skies clear, and the neighborhood quiet as we arrived about an hour before sundown on this winter evening. Mary got her recorder, and as is our custom, she headed off in one direction in search of EVP, and I in the other.

This cemetery is not large, and as usual, we kept each other in sight as we went about our separate meanderings.

I noticed right away that my electrical field measuring devices were indicating a higher than normal ambient reading of magnetic fields in the area. The readings at this moment were not necessarily typical of ghostly activity, and I suspected a man-made source. Sure enough, as I moved along towards the edge of the cemetery border,and the readings increased in strength, I spied the row of poles supporting electrical supply lines to the homes in the area. The field was strong, and got stronger as I approached the poles.

Whenever we find genuine paranormal activity, (particularly when apparitions, or ghosts, are perceived), it is common to note measurable fluctuations in magnetic field activity. Usually, these flucuations occur in concert with the paranormal event, and researchers believe that magnetic field activity is an important aspect of the paranormal and needs further study. Some researchers report that psychic and haunting activity is more prevalent in areas where higher ambient readings are noted, and on some occasions have found geological sources for these readings that coincide with localized paranormal activity. Studies are ongoing, and we anxiously await the results of more research coming our way in the future.At any rate, we watch for EVP and any ghostly phenomena with, or without magnetic field aberations. As it turns out, we had a fairly quiet visit this day with respect to ghostly activity.

Except for just one thing...........just one, single, lonely cowboy voice whispering in Mary's ear....... "YEE HAW !"...

"Yee Haw?" I exclaimed later as I replayed Mary's digital recording! In a whisper?

If you live in Texas, or perhaps in a rural area in many areas of the south, the cowboy slang exclamation "YEE HAW" can be heard above the general din of most any outdoor barbeque, sporting event, or social gathering where boisterous behavior is the norm. ....But a whisper?

"He likes me," said Mary, a woman of few words..... And I suppose one would just have to accept that notion under the circumstance.

This turned out to be a notable occasion in our EVP experiences where Mary is concerned. We have since taken serious note of the fact that EVP voices are commonly acquired by Mary in a whisper voice. Thus far, approximately 75% of her EVP recordings appear in a whisper. And, another thing, so far (knock on wood) Mary has never recorded any inappropriate remark, vulgarity or sexual inuendo (except for a little flirting), and generally speaking, the nature of her recordings has been messages of relative calm, peace, and thoughtful contemplation. I must say that my EVP experience has been quite different, as I frequently capture swearing voices and angry exclamations along with the usual peaceful and pleasant messages. I hope this situation continues, but in reality, we believe that sooner or later some "wise guy" spirit will spoil Mary's record. Meantime, we will try to promote only loving and peaceful thoughts around Mary while recording.

At this point we have no proven explanation for the peaceful nature of her EVP experiences, except to say that Mary is inwardly the most gentle and sweet person I've known. And many people who study the paranormal, myself included, firmly believe that when emotional and mental energies are released to the spiritual plane, they have a tendency to recieve similar energies in return. In other words, if you transmit fear, or anger when in a position of communicating with the spirit planes, then you must be prepared to attract the same in return. So, there is a strong case for purging ones mind of "unpleasant" emotion before indulging in any paranormal communication, particularly EVP.

"COWBOY GHOST" follows us home

That evening, as we looked over our collected data and photos from the approximately one hour visit to the cemetery, we reflected on the days events and found that the entire trip had only produced one noteworthy paranormal event, and that would be Mary's whispering voice. My EVP recorder produced not one single EVP, and that is an extremely rare occurance for me. I wondered if the high ambient magnetic fields had anything to do with this, but our attention would be quickly diverted later that night to an unfolding of events involving Mary, and the voice from the days visit to Alta Loma Cemetery.

Late that night, Mary was awakened from a sound sleep, and through sleepy eyes, she was shocked to see a man standing in the doorway of the bedroom!
"I was murdered" stated the apparition, matter of factly.

The male ghost appeared to be perhaps in his late twenties, with dark hair, boots, and rather plain pants and flannel shirt. Abruptly, Mary sprang to a heightened state of alertness, and the man faded away.

The next morning, reflecting upon the remarkable event of the previous night, Mary sat on the front porch enjoying her morning coffee and the relative peace and quiet after getting the kids off to school. The words spoken by the intruding male seemed to increase in intensity in her mind. She was convinced this message now repeating in her mind was a message with strength and purpose separate from her own thoughts. Was this entity trying to communicate?

"Listen to me," seemed to be the overwhelming feeling as Mary's senses became focused on the voice in her head.

And so, Mary got up and did what she and I always do.....she grabbed her digital recorder!

Mary began to speak aloud, encouraging the spirit entity to talk. She asked this spirit to try to speak to her and say what was on his mind. Mary decided to stay outside the house with the recorder, since the wave of intuition had come over her as she sat outside in the quiet of the morning. As she strolled under the trees around the house, the recorder silently collected any and all strong spiritual signals from the ether. Mary sensed a frustration within the energy that had come to her from the visit to the cemetary.

Returning to the house later in the day, I was filled in on the details of the nights events, and the daytime EVP session by Mary. She hadn't had time in the hustle and bustle of the mornings household duties to discuss it with me, as I had left early that morning.

We both were anxious to hear the EVP, so we took the first opportunity to load the audio into the digital analysis systems incorporated into our extensive computer lab in the house. Two separate computer set ups, with redundant back up systems, remote back up hard drive storage, CD recorder, printers, scanners, and multiple software audio filtering and analysis systems take up an entire 16 foot wall in a room in the house. Monitors jut out from wall mountings and loom over the keyboards and work stations. VCR networks, taperecorders, satelite TV distribution, video cameras, telephone recording apparatus, oscilloscopes, and a confusing mass of cable and wiring hook ups line the walls behind and beneath the gear..At least a dozen clip boards, calendars, note pads, a blackboard, baskets and CD storage racks hang from the walls. There is scarcely room to squeeze in a business card on remaining space upon the wall behind the work stations.

Finally, after about an hour of processing the 5 minute recording acquired by Mary that morning, sounds of voices began to emerge. A weak, frustrating, almost chanting cadence to the voice appeared repeating the same words, in variable, brief, groupings........

"number...." "the numbers....." "it's the numbers...." whispered the voice over and over.....

Yes, the voice was talking to Mary, as it was at the cemetery, in a whisper. But this time, it was not a flirting, "cowboy" quip, but some intense, repetition with a definite frustrated tone...

"numbers, the number....the numbers..." and then the weak voice faded away.

What on earth did this cryptic message mean? Were we hearing clues to the frustration of a spirit who was forced to exit this life before his time? Mary immediately asked me to accompany her to the cemetery to follow up on this baffling information.
At this juncture, my mood flowed to quiet contemplation momentarily and after a long pause I said.... "Mary, we need to talk about this one for a minute......"

You see, at this point, Mary had been experiencing some very distressing health problems. It had only recently been learned that Mary's heart murmer, which she had for years, had suddenly began to get worse. A major valve in her heart was failing, and she was growing weaker and would be soon scheduled for a critical surgery. Events were complicated by three (count 'em) bouts of hospitalization in 4 months with a persistant and debilitating case of pneumonia. I felt that an intense encounter with an entity bearing a message about murder and possible intrigue should be avoided for now to prevent undue pressure and anxiety for Mary. So, with a little pressure from myself, Mary agreed to curtail this rather intensive and escalating scenario until she regained her strength.

"Anyways," said myself with a wink, "who does this guy think he is coming into our bedroom at night like that? What if we had been... ?.......well, you know........oh, never mind........"

Later, in March of 2003, an amazing fact was revealed at a getogether of the local historical society at the Railroad museum on Hwy 6 in Santa Fe. "Say Rich," announced one of the local old timers at the meetin', " I guess you knew that the very first person to be buried in the Alta Loma Cemetery was a murder victim? You knew that, didn't 'cha...?"

Hmmmmm, well, you know, I guess I did know that already, didn't I? heh, heh. One thing Mary and I have learned is that spirits have no fear of telling the truth. It can't hurt them anymore, you know. They usually get right to the point in their messages.

As I now relate this story for the book, Mary has had her surgery, and an artificial device was put into her heart to replace the defective valve. She is recuperating nicely, and maybe someday we'll return to the Alta Loma Cemetery to seek the answer to the frustrations of the "whispering cowboy." But, you know...sometimes I think perhaps we should leave it as is..... The ghost told Mary he was murdered, and we have since learned a murder victim mentioned by historians was, in fact, the very first burial at that cemetery. In that case, if this is the "Whispering Cowboy", then he probably considers himself a ghostly celebrity, and might occasionally take a "liking" to certain visitors at the cemetery......

And, of course, as Mary says.... "He likes me..."

016- YEE HAW

017- MARY

Who Are Those Guys, Anyway?

Years ago, there was a great movie starring Robert Redford and Paul Neuman called "Butch Cassidy and the Sundance Kid." Redford and Neuman (Butch and Sundance) spent most of the movie humorously evading an eternally persistant group of lawmen, led by one who seemed to unerringly know just where to look for the two hapless outlaws. At many points in the never ending chase, the two characters would thoughtfully look at each other, perhaps after gazing back at the dust cloud on the horizon which always contained the determined lawmen, and then one of them would calmly state to the other "Who are those guys, anyway?"

I can't tell you how many times I myself have spoken those words quietly to myself as I went through the analysis and processing of Electronics Voice Phenomena (EVP). I have certainly recorded a diverse group of voices, and always found fascinating differences in the data from these EVP voices from each selected locale.

Who are those guys, anyway.......?

Let me just give you the short answer to that question for now, and as we proceed in this book with our adventures in electronics voice phenomena, hopefully you will be inspired to later do some of your own personal study on the spiritual implications of the experiences discussed in this book.

For the most part, most researchers and investigators pretty much agree that when we die, we are quickly disassociated from our physical bodies and find ourselves in spirit form. In spirit form we are aware and seemingly quite in control of ourselves, in spite of the fact that we can not be heard or seen by our loved ones on earth. No doubt, this can be a rude awakening for most. Some folks who have held rigid belief systems of life and death, or those who may have not given much thought at all to spiritual things, will find that they need assistance and time to adjust to the reality of their new existence.

Most researchers, psychics, and others who have experienced out of body experiences (OBE's), and near death experiences (NDE's), say that there will be guides, friends, deceased family, etc., to assist during this time. However, it is up to the individual to open themselves to this help, and many require "spiritual time" or a "period of adjustment" to accept this concept of their new reality. Individual spirits will require different lengths of time to adjust, and almost all agree that even the most enlightened spirits will at least briefly visit their loved ones (and even attend their own funeral,) before moving on to higher levels of spiritual planes.

And there you have it....... "Who are those guys?" is explained then, I believe, by the presence of a diverse group of spirits in a sort of "interim level or plane" situated in and around the earth plane.This level would seem to be the origin of most EVP. Some spirits here have recently passed on, some have been at that level for some time and find themselves in a position to be of service to others there, some are indeed lost or otherwise still confused, and then another whole unknown group of spirits with specific purpose may be found. Many of those would be defined as guides, helpers, or angels. Others may not have even lived in a body on earth. I suppose we won't know all the details until.....well, you know.

I have learned to be very careful what I say when I am seeking EVP recordings. I always announce to the spirits what my purpose is, and explain to them what I can and can't do. It is necessary to make these statements as briefly as possible. There is every indication that any reply or communication from a spirit using this method will always be brief. Most researchers think there may be some energy requirement which must be adhered to, and we always find the messages to be short and to the point.

Until I learned to be very careful about what I say in these sessions, I once had the misfortune of finding that I might have mislead some of the spirits who had answered me. In one case, in a cemetery (as an afterthought), I had simply asked if any spirits had any messages. Later while processing the audio, I discovered an immediate response from an entity who asked me to say hello to a certain Pastor, and also to a lady (whose first names were both given.) I was horrified to think that I may have given a false promise to this spirit, as I had no chance of figuring out who these people were or giving this message to them. In several other cases, spirits have cried out to me to help them. Of course, I was not able at that exact moment to even hear them, and I had neglected to explain that point to them when I requested their communication.

Now when I do an EVP session, my every word is planned and rehearsed according to the objectives and location of the session. I want to make sure I don't say something to disturb a spirit entity or mislead them. After all, I'd just as soon not upset someone and have them follow me home or something.

My experiences with EVP have proven to me that beyond a doubt there is a dimensional existence beyond our life on earth. My life, my values, and beliefs have all changed for the better, as I have become more aware of this spiritual knowledge.

Spirits In The Hood

THE HOMELESS, CAUGHT IN AN ENDLESS CYCLE

Rich takes EVP recorders and camera into the streets to capture spirit voices surrrounding the homeless and prostitutes on the streets!

The homeless population on the city streets of America has grown tremendously in recent years. Is this just the product of an "out of control" population explosion that has resulted in our earth being overrun like an ant bed? Or are there other factors, perhaps economical, social, or medical, at work here? Studies show that the chronically homeless are afflicted with disabilities that are among the worst for humans to cope with on their own; such as mental illness, and alcohol and drug addiction. Many chronically homeless suffer from all three. And what would you say came first, as a "chicken or the egg" scenario? Well, in the opinion of the health care and social workers I interviewed, most people get it entirely wrong. Booze and drugs are not at the heart the problem.

If we allow ourselves to be swayed by the never ending "war on drugs," and the Hollywood and TV image of the drunk on the street with a wine bottle,we would all assume the homeless to just be a stoned group of ne'er do wells hell bent on their next drink or their next fix. But according to social workers that I talked with, they will tell you without hesitation that the main difficulty is mental illness, and that other factors are only a result of their inability to cope as normal folks do.

Why, you ask, then is that such a problem? It would seem that we have a system for treating mental illness just as we treat those who have other illness and can't pay......right? Well,....no, actually, we do not. There is a "catch 22" that is responsible for returning every mentally ill person to the street just about as fast as it is determined that a person is in need of help.

You see, the quandry is that a mentally ill person usually is incapable of realizing that he or she is ill, and therefore will almost always refuse treatment. And the LAW states, that no person can be hospitalized without their own consent and permission. Now, think about that for just a second, and then as we continue with more on this absurd situation created by a bungling bureaucracy, the dilema unfolds....

Now here is the other part of the issue...When a person finally, (through pressure from friends, family, or the law), admits themselves for treatment for mental illness, the state operated facilities will release them when they are stabilized with medication. Usually, most patients are pushed out the door after less than two weeks. Then they are considered "well" and must obtain medication and continue to treat themselves.

"Aha," you say, "but wait a minute"..... When they take the meds, and they begin to feel better, (remember... as a symptom of their illness they can't usually recognize that they are in fact ill) then, of course, they feel fine so they STOP taking their meds. And here we go again. In a few more weeks, they have spiraled downhill and have wound up right back where they started. It is a vicious never ending cycle.

Decades ago, before tranquilizers were discovered as a treatment for mental illness, many seriously ill patients were all but lost in huge sanitariums where they may virtually be incarcerated for most of their lives. In an effort to change that situation, new laws were enacted to prevent patients from hospitalization against their will. Now, they are on the streets with their illness and none of them can tell you why. So much for mixing the government bureaucracy and medicine. They obviously still haven't found the solution.....

ONWARD TO THE STREETS

I pulled the car over at the corner of the Salvation Army building and started to chat with John and James (two homeless men), who were hoping someone would stop by and offer them a days work.

James was more than eager to tell me of his many experiences with the paranormal. Although John also had one story to tell, he good naturedly fell into the role of poking fun at James' exuberance as James was telling me his stories.

As James paused from his narrative only for a split second, a spirit voice cried out for "HELP" in the brief pause on the recording. We were quite alone, and it was a very quiet morning in the "hood." We didn't hear a thing although this voice seems to be screaming....In this recording, you can also hear James and John kidding around before and after the spirit voice....

018- "HELP"

With more of John's good natured ribbing,and in the middle of James's long winded ghost tale, it seems that a spirit decided to get in on the humor of the situation....

019- "Ya heard that old Crap!"

After horsing around with James and John for about 10 minutes, it occurred to me that our lively discussion might be interfering with their prospects of being offered a job, so I slipped them each enough money to buy them a good breakfast, and moved on.

OPERATION EVP "STING" BEGINS

I headed away from the main street location of the Salvation Army HQ, and pointed my Toyota Corolla towards the east end of Galveston Island. I would seek conversation with folks on the street along the waterfront, and the seawall, if any could be located.

It was around 10 am on a week day February morning, and the skies were dreary and overcast. As temperatures were in the fifties, conditions on the street were not exactly miserable by some peoples' standards, but might just be a bit uncomfortable for anyone to just be "hanging out" on the seawall today. Since, I was already here though, I would give it a try. I drove along the back streets of east end, and, seeing no one, I headed for the more "touristy" section of the seawall boulevard.

No sooner than I hit the seawall, I spied activity around a vehicle pulled over to the curb side. Two women, dressed in short skirts and heels and such were beside the car. One leaned over the window of the drivers side conversing with the occupant. The other immediately noticed my attention being directed towards them, and quickly turned toward the street facing me and waved. As I slowly passed, she leaned forward in order to see into the window of the low profile Toyota, and smiled.

"All right!" I exclaimed to myself..... "I've got one...................Now what do I do?"

My attention lurched away from the rear view mirror, and back to the task of driving the car. I spied a street intersection coming right up, and decided to turn in and go around the block. I spot checked my gear. My vest had my press tag and ID card in plain view, and my very best "wire" recorder was tucked in underneath my shirt and vest, and the tiny microphone fastened to button on my shirt. My camera was "locked and loaded."

"Operation EVP Sting" was about to be launched!

As I turned on the side street to go around the block, I met a slight obstacle.....this was not a through street. No problem.....it will take more than this to deter me from my objective ! I swung the car around, headed back to the intersection, and promptly met face to face with a police cruiser.

"Holy $%!!?*"....I muttered...I hadn't thought about this possibility. What if these guys had come along as I was pulling up to talk with these fine ladies on the street corner?

I began to construct my reply to the police in my mind.... " But Officer.... "It's not what you think... you see....I have a perfectly good explanation for this!" I instantly realized how the officers would take my explanation of recording spirit voices while mingling with these scantily clad gals!! Laughing out loud at my own self, I decided to rethink this operation before proceeding!

The police cruiser pulled through a convenience store parking lot, and slowly returned to the street heading back in the direction from which it came. Obviously, they had no interest in me, but I had received a momentary dose of paranoia and I decided I would use this to my advantage.

I followed the cruiser, and at the first opportune moment, I flagged down the squad car.

" Holy $%!!?*" I once more uttered under my breath. "I've lost my mind....am I really pulling over a police car?"

"Yep," was my obvious answer, and I got out of my car, somewhat nervously approaching the police vehicle with my hands where they could see them.

"Hey guys," I blurted........ Um, I really don't have any emergency, I just wanted to ask you a question....er....hope you don't mind."

I approached the side front window, bent down on the curb side and began to try to make myself not look stupid as I spoke.... "I'm a free lance writer and photographer, and I'm doing a piece on the homeless and people who are living or make a living on the streets. I figured you would know where I might go in order to maybe nail down a couple of homeless folks so's I could interview them."

"Oh yeah, no problem" said the officer by the curb side window. He smiled, and I gave a huge "silent sigh of relief" at that critical moment. I noticed the other more stern faced officer running my vehicle license plate on his computer. (Sheesh, gimme a break) "Why, thank you officer" I smiled with what must have seemed a phony smile, "I hated to bother you guys, but I figured you could tell me what areas to avoid for safety's sake." "Sure, good idea," he replied,and he proceeded to tell me a couple of the best places.... the Salvation Army (which I had only just left), and the homeless shelter called "Our Daily Bread."

Then I inserted into the conversation the real reason for my pulling this police car over to the side .... "Hey thanks for that information guys....oh...yeah...and by the way....I guess this boulevard is more or less your regular beat, huh?

"Yep," came the brief reply.

"OK,......ummmm, I er...ahh...will be including in some of those interviews, possibly er...ummm a quick talk with a prostitute or two. (Did I just say that to a cop?) And it occurred to me that you fellas might just see me along the road here and I wouldn't, you know,want you to more or less misinterpret my intentions. heh, heh....know what I mean?"

The cop who had previously smiled, looked to his left at the stern faced cop, and they both broke into a laugh.... "Knock yerself out," said the one nearest me. "Whatever rings your bells" added stoneface, "just use good sense about where you go and what you do. Some of those types ain't your real upstanding citizens, you know."

I thanked them, and asked them a quick question about a tent I had seen back in some palmettos along the waterfront. "Belongs to an old homeless fella thats lived along there for about five years now," was the reply, "he moves to high ground during rainy spells, and back again when the weather straightens out."

I stepped back feeling as though I had made life long friends with them, thanked them again, and away they went.

As I mused over the apparent success of my license plate check, and simultaneously fretted over the preposterous notion that a homeless man was living for five years in a tent within sight of the majority of citizens of this community, I jumped back in the car and tried to re focus on my objectives.

Pulling back into traffic, I hurried towards the previous location of the chicks with the short skirts. I now had permission from the cops to visit with a prostitute! Onward with "Operation EVP Sting!"

Nearing the end of the boulevard and scouring each corner as I went along, I suddenly realized that the very spot along the curb which had held my objective, was empty. No cars, no short skirts....nothing.

"Holy $%!!?*", I exclaimed again, for the third time in just a few minutes. This operation may not be as easy as I had thought.........

IF AT FIRST YOU DON'T SUCCEED......

My next chance to cruise the boulevards of Galveston came a couple months later, in late April. Spring had "sprung," and the oleanders and other various flowering tropical and sub tropical blooms were in full color. Day temperatures were already getting well into the eighties, and the tourists were showing up by the numbers.

Mary's health had continued to be bothersome during the winter, and on this day I had dropped her off at the hospital for a consultation with her doctor. I had some time to kill, so I headed for the Sea Wall boulevard. I had read an article in the paper about a psychic who had opened a shop on the strip, and I would see if I could find it.The story was this lady had used her psychic abilities while doing work with the CIA. Sounded interesting....and in the back of my mind was nailed down the necessity to also get that interview with a street prostitute today.

I never have been very fond of the "worlds oldest profession." It always seemed to me to be rather a demeaning prospect for a lonely man to have to pay for female company..... But drama of this sort is the "stuff" of life, and there is no doubt that all areas of emotion...love, hate, despair, loneliness, joy, confusion...(you name it), can all probably be found in the aura of life surrounding a single prostitute on any single given day.

According to the article I read about the psychic store, it would be found located at the front of the old Balinese Room, a historical restaurant building on an old pier at the east end of the island. As I drove along looking for the old pier, my mind drifted back to the subject of prostitution.. One eye on the street looking for a short skirt and high heels, and one eye on the street looking for an old pier.

Mentally, my mind "blinked" suddenly to a forgotten memory. A hazy recollection of a young man in a Navy uniform (guess who) walking along a downtown Naples, Italy, street on an evening somewhere in the 60's. By myself, bored and lonely, I made eye contact with a young, shapely, dark eyed beauty with a soft smile. In a magic moment, we just burst into conversation as if we had planned all along to meet here on the street. Speaking broken

English, but doing a decent job of communicating, she engaged me in small talk as we strolled along.

I was clueless.

Somehow, in a matter of only a few minutes, and a couple of turns down increasingly smaller streets, I found myself in front of a door in an alley, standing behind this female benefactor to my loneliness, as she put a key into the door lock. The door swung open, and then shut, with the pair of us now inside the tiny dwelling.

She turned on a soft light, and my young and naive 20 year old brain was assaulted with the reality of life on the streets of remote and unknown corners of the world. As I slowly turned in one spot, and surveyed the interior, I realized that I was in a single room, about 10 feet square, with a tiny toilet area in what seemed to be a closet. A sink, and a small refrigerator about 4 feet high next to it, a bed, a dresser and a couple of other undetermined small pieces of furniture.

I barely had a chance to complete my survey of the room, when she pulled off her coat, plopped down on the tiny bed, and said "Hey, you give me five dollars?"

With the request for the money, and no more fanfare whatsoever, she fell back on the bed, lifted up her hips, grabbed her skirt on the sides with both hands, and using her thumbs and forefingers gently inched up her skirt along her thighs towards her waist. She had not actually yet removed even a single article of clothing (except her jacket.) My eyes riveted to this action, (well, what did you expect me to do?), I watched as it was revealed that she was wearing no underclothing whatsoever, and, furthermore, she was completely shaven as well. Both of these issues got the better of my attention for sure, but in no way was I prepared for what I saw next.......

From the corner of my eye, and from the direction that I was previously looking before being interrupted by the not-so-subtle activities of the dark eyed babe on the bed, I spied a small piece of furniture that I had missed in my brief scan of the room.

A tiny cradle. A very tiny bassinette type baby bed, with, are you ready for this....a tiny newborn baby......sound asleep, and quite oblivious of the harshness of the adult scene unfolding in the cramped room.

I was stunned. My young mind raced with the stark reality of the scene that materialized before me. Over the space of just a few seconds, I gained light years of maturity as the pieces of the puzzle fell together...right down to and including the fact that this babe (the adult one) was freshly shaven. My mind was on overload as I felt compassion for the plight of the young lady, and at the same time, hurt and embarrassment at my own lack of worldly knowledge as I stupidly fell into this lair of male human weakness.

I reached in my pocket, pulled out a fiver (American money, please) and handed it to her as I mumbled, "sorry." I quickly headed for the door as she called out after me.... "hey baby...you no fuck me?" Out the door I went, and into the night with my thoughts. That was the first time in at least a year I had been that close to the naked private parts of a woman (well, you know, there hadn't actually been that many times before that either) but, believe me, this time it just didn't do a thing for me. On the one hand, I was amazed at myself for having walked out, but on the other hand, the sheer desperation of this human drama had outweighed all instincts.

With this piece of personal history uppermost in my mind, my thoughts wandered back to the task at hand and I wondered how I would react to a face to face meeting with a prostitute at this much later stage in my life. "Piece of cake," I mused as I continued my search for a pier, or a memory, whichever would come first.

The pier came first....there it was "The Balinese Room", and then I spied the small sign at the front of the building for the psychic shop. Along the side of the store was a four foot long white banner with red letters ... "OPEN", it said. Well, that was lucky, since it was only 10 AM and Galveston Island is usually slow to wake up in the mornings.

I opened one of my cases and pulled out a digital recorder to see if I could pick up any comments from the usual peanut gallery of spirit voices that accompany me almost everywhere anymore. After parking, locking up, and walking a half block back to the pier and the psychic shop, I navigated the steps to the front door, grabbed the handle and pulled. Nothing. Standing back a foot or so, I surveyed the door. A "closed" sign lay at an odd angle across the inside in the shadows. I peeked through the glass, and no one was there. I turned, walked back down the steps and glanced at the huge "OPEN" sign on the side of the store. I wanted to write "sometimes" on it, but it was out of reach. Mumbling to myself, I headed back to the car.

I resolved myself to get on with the other part of my goals for the day.....it was time to cruise the streets and find some action !

Apparently, I was not the only one who was anxious for some "action" ! Remember my comment about the "peanut gallery" back at the pier? When scanning my recordings of those few minutes, I learned that I had picked up two boisterous spirits who had attached themselves to my task of locating a hooker. Like two kibitzing comedians, they seemed to be having a great time looking for prostitutes too! One voice referred to the other as "Bennie," and Bennie had a high pitched comical voice, and seemed quite without patience.........

"Bennie...that's a whore!!.. "exclaimed one of the spirits.." Calm down, you queer!!"...screamed the comical voice of Bennie...then........" Bennie, that's a Ho!!" protested the spirit voice once again to Bennie!

020- "Bennie, that's a whore !"

The antics of Bennie and company would hopefully set the mood for a light hearted encounter with a "working girl." or so I hoped anyway. But with the spirit world in tow, it could easily happen that other more serious statements may have to be made as well....

Rich scores...an interview, that is !.....

I guess Bennie and his cohorts were guiding me as I zipped down the boulevard. In no time, (maybe only a minute or so), I spied a female form, alone on the street, and seemingly intent on inspecting the drivers of vehicles as they passed. I got my share of her attention as I passed, and I quickly made a u-turn hoping to not miss this opportunity.

I pulled up against the curb, overlooking the surf and directly across the street from the lady in question. Her appearance was not the usual for a street hooker, but then maybe summertime in the Galveston beach area calls for a different uniform. She wore sandals, blue jean shorts, and a sleeveless top. A red bandana tied around her hair, and she looked pretty much like any other girl strolling along the sidewalk. Except for that "something" about her, like maybe the way she walks, or the way she makes eye contact with too many men who are passing.

She had seen me make a u-turn, and was watching for me as I returned. From across the street, we smiled at each other as I rolled down the window. She strolled across the boulevard, and came around to the front passenger side of the car. I reached across and lifted the handle, swinging open the door in an inviting manner.

Instantly, as was later revealed by our EVP digital recordings, the spirits blended into the scenery, and began to make observations and comments as my conversations began.

"Hi, how are you ?" I spoke to the girl as she pulled the door to her.

"Oh, pretty good..." was the reply from the approaching hooker....and then........

"We're afraid" said a second female voice drearily, followed by an astounding third female voice with a dry, sarcastic wit, who quipped; "Dead, as always!"

Whoa.!...wait a minute....What was this? I had distinctly different answers to my greeting, from several different female voices at the same time! What could this mean? Did the hooker have spirit friends along with her? It seemed by the way the other voices answered my greeting, that the spirits thought they were being addressed by me as well...! And then there was the part about "dead as always." Hmmm, that one could produce a few goosebumps under the right conditions!

021- "How are you ?".... "We're afraid"..... "Dead, as always !"

The spirit crowd gathering around my vehicle seemed to be growing. I assumed weird Bennie and his buddy were closely observing us, and before another word was spoken by myself or the prostitute, a male voice offered his encouragement to the girl to get in the car.....

022- "Pick-up baby," "pretty girl"

It would seem that my project was attracting a good bit of attention in the spirit world!

Her name was "Candy," although, of course, that wasn't her real name. She seemed to have little ambition or goals, and was not currently on drugs, although she certainly had her share of drug usage in the past. In fact, at 29 years old, she was now enrolled in a program at a local hospital where researchers routinely monitored her for drug usage and tested her for the dreaded diseases which are the current plague of the street people....AIDS, hepatitis, and others. She had been clean for two years, practiced safe sex (condoms), and was getting paid for her participation in the study. Although she said that she further lessened her risk by trying to develop a "regular" clientele whom she could "get to know better and trust," I could not help but wonder when her luck would run out and her life be threatened by the loathsome virus of careless sex. At this point I considered the observations of the social workers concerning their opinion that the mental illness was the common underlying cause, not the drugs. In this case, it appeared that Candy's issues could indeed be associated with her inability to deal with certain realities of life, and further demonstrated, (if we can believe her testimony,) by the fact that in her case the drugs were not now as much of a problem as other more complex psychological issues in her life.

My recorder was of course, running along as we chatted....I had immediately told her about the recorder, that I was a free lance writer, and my only purpose for our visit was an interview, and NOT to have sex. She seemed a little suspicious at first, and said she didn't want to do anything that would get her into trouble. After a few minutes of conversation, I had convinced her that I was not part of an undercover sting, and that all we really were going to do is talk. She seemed then more comfortable, and even told me a story about her and a girlfriend playing around with a Ouija board and causing some strange reaction with flashing lights appearing about the room. But other than that single story, she had not much experience with the paranormal. I think her world was, at least for the moment, fairly well defined by the isolation and desperation of her lifestyle and profession.

She asked for a cigarette, and I explained that I did not smoke. At that point I slipped her a ten spot for her time, and suggested that would buy her some smokes. Momentarily, she spied a vehicle slowly driving by her corner, and she quickly snapped from her brief interlude with the interview and told me she had been watching for that guy this morning...a "friend" she said.......

Immediately I took the cue and sent her on her way, thanking her for her time. We had spent 11 minutes talking in the front seat of the car. "I'll watch for your book", she yelled as she dashed across the traffic and back to her corner of the world. With the traffic on one side of my car, and the pounding surf just beyond the sea wall on the other, I wondered what the recordings would be like. Probably a lot of background noise, I thought. I was correct on that one as it turned out, but was still able to turn out some very interesting comments from the spirit dimension and was relieved that, finally, I had scored my interview with a lady of the night. Even if it was the daytime.

Here is an irreverent EVP which showed up during my little talk with Candy on the sea wall of Galveston Island. You will find in my chapter on the "Fish Group" an explanation, and stories about the voices spoken by those referred to as "Fish." This is a typical demonstration of such messages, although there was no particular reference to the Fish Group in this case. Nevertheless, this EVP voice definitely was appealing to the "dark" side as he encouraged me to take advantage of my proximity to the hookers and the overall environment, as he frustratingly shouted

023- "Go fuck one...shit!"

Finishing up the interview, the comments grew more numerous, and more to the point. Reminding me of a group of "hard hats" standing around with not much to do except root for their own side of the issue, the following string of comments from several male voices seemed to be perfect for concluding this part of the story.......

024- "Really......that's a Ho.."..... "Your pussy now?..".... "That's obscene !"

Needless to say, some spirit voices do not seem to show much embarrassment, while others will seem to be the picture of propriety. Honesty and forthright and bold statements are usually the order of the day, and when the subject is sex and hookers......brace yourself for a blast of reality. The spirits will speak their minds........

A Pet Story

Mary and Rex, our very own 80lb angel

We all love our pets, and most of us accept and love them as regular members of the family. Almost all of us cherish the memory of a loved pet from our childhood, and pets have provided immeasurable comfort and companionship for disabled folks and the elderly. We have always admired their keen abilities of the senses, and many miraculous tales are told of pets who have performed unbelievable acts of courage and demonstrated amazing feats of unusual instinctive behavior (particularly regarding loyalty to their owners and human family members.) Many mediums and paranormal researchers believe that pets are "teachers" for us, and are commonly found at the side of their masters in the afterlife.

I have always loved animals, and have even been in the pet business. I have owned pet shops and boarding and grooming kennels,and I have an interesting paranormal story about a dog for you....

Way back in the early eighties, a customer brought a stray puppy, about 6 months old, into my shop. She asked if I wanted to take this female stray. Not then even recognizable as a pure bred poodle, she was covered in mud, tangled matts, and even had a long tail. (Poodles tails are bobbed.) My partner was a veterinarian and occupied the space next to the pet shop. I took her in and had her checked over. She had heart worms, intestinal parasites, was undernourished and had obviously been lost and neglected.

After one long look into those big sad black eyes, and a lick on my chin, I admitted this very shy puppy into the veterinary hospital. Over the period of the next 3 months, with careful medical care and lots of loving,she was transformed into the most beautiful, healthy, velvet black poodle you've ever seen. Her temperament was extraordinary. She was very loving, laid back, and attentively watched every move of her new master...me ! She had obviously been mistreated previously, and was very shy. I named her "Spooky" because she seemed timid and jumpy. I took her to work at the shop every day, and she always attracted attention everywhere we went.

One thing was unusual about this dog. Most small dogs have a shrill, rather high pitched voice which results in a bark that would be described as a "yap." Not so with Spooky, her voice was deep and a bit raspy sounding. She had a habit of "woofing" to get your attention. She would quietly walk up to me when she wanted to go outside, and she would look up and go"woof, woof" ever so gently. It didn't sound like a bark, but sounded just like the word is spelled....."woof." Her bark was unique.

She was my constant companion at work and at play, and when (after my divorce in the mid 80's) I met Mary, it was no time at all until Mary accepted the unique gentle nature of this loving creature. Nearing her 17th year of life, Spooky finally acquired a form of cancer which we were not able to treat.

About a year after she died, she actually came back to us in a most extraordinary EVP event. She actually spoke to Mary and I, in her unique raspy little"woof" while on an EVP field trip alone in a quiet cemetery near home. In this beautiful lonely cemetery, on a still summers day, among giant oak trees laden with Spanish moss....a most extraordinary thing happened.....In an unmistakable "woof, woof, woof", (which I could pick out of a MILLION dog voices anywhere as the distinctive voice of our Spooky) she took that moment of solitude to remind us of our times together.....

025- WOOF WOOF WOOF

Actual digital recording of our pet as described in story above!

The Fish Group
THE "DEMONS OF EVP"

Writing about the "Fish Group" is not going to be easy. First of all, I want you to know that it's possible that I may somewhat regret writing this for any number of reasons, most of which you are about to learn...

You see....The Fish Group is .....well......I guess there is really no way to soften the effect of this information, it's better to just lay it on the line. The Fish Group is an actual group of EVP spirit voices, who can commonly appear in a most volatile, unfriendly, and frightening manner. Their language can be rough, vulgar, obscene, hateful, and designed to play upon the personal fears of the particular individual who is collecting the EVP samples. This can (and usually does), further extend to actual clairaudient phenomena with more experienced EVP experimenters. The Fish Group has been referred to by EVP experiencers as the

"Demons" of EVP. In some cases there have been reports of phenomenon increasing from EVP to actual apparitions, shadowy figures, and poltergeist type manifestations.

Now before anybody gets all in a panic over this, let me state in no uncertain terms that I have never personally seen, nor have I ever been told by any person, of a circumstance where an individual was physically harmed by the Fish Group or any other spirit group or single spirit entity while conducting an EVP session. Scared...well, yes...but not harmed.

And that is an issue which needs clarification before we continue. I personally have found that fear itself is the actual demon in any ghost or haunted encounter. I've not yet known anyone to be actually hurt by any type of paranormal encounter, but I do believe that such a thing could occur if one became so frightened that they lost control of their psychic well being. I have indeed been warned by many a paranormal investigator to be wary of being surprised and unprepared for any extreme supernatural situation. One interview with an internationally well known paranormal investigator of over 30 years, disclosed that in all his career, only once was he actually frightened...and that was when from inside a haunted house a board suddenly flew through the air and struck him on the head. It can happen...but it's rare.

I have stood alone in the darkness, (more than once), in the middle of the night, in a cemetary in a city that I had never visited before. Quite frankly, I believe that most of the time even while in a true haunted situation, that if a person maintains control over his mental state, he can not be taken advantage of. Perhaps, as in my case, a person's background and training can help. Things like learning meditation techniques, self hypnosis, physical fitness training, discipline training such as is received in military, aviation pilot school, scuba diving training and experience, etc., can all be helpful in keeping a clear head and avoiding panic when faced with frightening circumstances.

I have, of course, had my own experiences with the "Fish", and have discussed many contact reports from email of readers of my website, as well as members of the AAEVP. The American Association of EVP, founded by Sarah Estep, author of "Voices of Eternity", is a fine group, (of which I am a member), that seriously studies, discusses and compares notes of encounters with all types of EVP experiences. AAEVP members have a healthy respect for the Fish Group, and most strongly advise any contact with Fish to be quickly curtailed, and all further attempts at communication from them to be ignored.

The Fish seem to be pranksters, and can be considerably less than funny at their pranks. Typically, when a person picks up and records a Fish message, they can be curious about the language or tone of the message, and might make an attempt to re contact. It appears that the more contact is made, the stronger the language and the more frightening the return message becomes....even to a point of playing on secret fears of the unwitting participant. No one knows why they are this way, and curiously, when ignored for a long period of time, they eventually just go away! They usually just simply appear (in the same manner as spiteful or hurtful humans) to take advantage of people's weaknesses...sort of like "bullies on a playground."

In my case, with my first exposure to the Fish Group, they did indeed take advantage of a weakness of my own at that time. Mary had been seriously ill for almost a year and the illness had led to the discovery of a malfunctioning heart valve. She would need to have open heart surgery in order to replace the bad valve with a man-made device. During her weakness from the illness, her condition deteriorated and she contracted pneumonia and was hospitalized three times.

At only 48 years young, she was suffering a serious health set back which would result in about a two year period of great worry for Mary, myself, and the whole family.

One night, just before her surgery and during a rather fitfull night of difficulty sleeping, I awoke from a momentary slumber, and lie awake getting up the energy to mosey into the bathroom. Down the hall, and into the living room, our fifty gallon aquarium was gently humming away from the filter motor, the bubbles were gently gurgling and could be easily heard in the still of the night. Also, in the living room,the blades of a small fan lazily turned, adding to an overall moderate level of ambient noise.

Anyone who has had any level of experience with clairaudient phenomena as a result of working with EVP, will recognize immediately this type of noise level source as a precurser to not only random and common clairaudient ghostly voices, but indeed as a favorite "energy source" of the despised Fish Group. Suddenly, over the gentle purring of the aquarium and fan noise, I heard a constant, and most emphatic male voice ranting and on the verge of shouting. It reminded me very much of an old fashioned revival, hell fire and brimstone type preacher!
What the hell...?? I thought...and at this moment due to my experience with EVP, I quickly recognized the familiar timbre, tempo, and cadence of the ghostly voice superimposed over the steady mechanical sounds. Instead of jumping up and losing the benefit of my concentration, I lay still and tried to discern his words. The tirade seemed too busy for me to translate, but suddenly   the   voice   paused,   and   shouted "DIE...DIE...DIE....DIE!! and then launched back into that absolute barrage of insane banter and ranting for a few seconds. Momentarily,   the   voice   again   paused   and   shouted "DIE...DIE...DIE."

"Enough!!...Dammit!" I threw back the covers and headed forthwith towards the living room aquarium and its outrageous source of midnight nit wittery, and fully prepared myself to do battle with this outrageous loudmouth.

Upon coming face to face with the aquarium, all that was to be found was a peaceful and serene bubbling tank of water with some tropical fish somewhat annoyed at me for disturbing their evening. "Man, whats going on here?" I fumed, and resumed my trip to the bathroom and shortly thereafter, went back to sleep.

Two nights later.... I awakened much as before, lazily dreading having to trek all the way to the bathroom, when again, from the living room aquarium, came the very same raging voice, pausing as before and shouting "DIE...DIE...DIE...!" This time I threw back the covers, headed for the closet and pulled out my audio investigators hard case and grabbed a digital recorder. "I'll teach 'em..." I fretted. Not known to me at the time, I was indeed falling right into the "Fish trap." I was playing their game, and setting myself up to be the brunt of their folly. I cranked up a digital recorder, placed it on the fish tank, and went back to bed. It was quiet, and again I was asleep in no time.

At this point you are no doubt wondering if the name "Fish Group" has anything to do with the fish tank which seemed to be the source of the disruptive voice. Actually, communication from EVP voices tells us that the Fish Group likes to compare themselves to fish in a tank, while observing us in our respective dimensional reality. "We are Fish...we watch you." is in fact a direct quote from a Fish message. The Fish Group may, in fact, find themselves somewhat without explanation for their quandry, and may be spiteful towards us for having the apparent freedom that may have been lost to them. Actually, in this case, it would be they who could have the "real" freedom...they apparently just haven't realized it yet and don't know how to move on spiritually from their present position. Animosity seems to be a human failing which the Fish have retained in their sport. Indeed, they can be just plain RUDE!

The next morning, I checked over the recordings and found that the loud mouth "Preacher" was not on the tape, nor was the "DIE" message. However, a steady stream of random conversation tidbits could be discerned. There was a lot of swearing, and some of the dialogue sounded like recordings of people arguing and yelling at each other. Very strange...and in this case, as I had conducted this session in my sleepiness and aggravated state and without planning, the recordings were audible but far from optimum. Not likely to make good reproductions for public use on the internet or CD.

It was at this point I contacted a few of my friends and discussed the Fish, and a few tactics for dealing with them. In general, the best way, most agree, is to avoid and ignore them. They seek attention.

The following night I awoke, as usual, and lie there again waiting to get the energy to get up and go to the bathroom and take a leak. No noise from the aquarium....that's a relief....

Suddenly, with a strength so great that I felt the actual sound percussion on the side of my face, a voice emanated from within the bed itself, as if coming from a point suspended in mid air between Mary and I. It firmly exclaimed... "DEATH !" I almost jumped out of my skin, and immediately reached for Mary. I felt her chest to see if she was breathing....the thing I feared most for the better part of the last year was sumed up in this single fearsome word which had come to me from nowhere in the middle of the night.

"Damn Fish! DAMMIT !" I shouted. Mary rolled over and with barely enough waking energy to muster a "what the...".......

"Nothin' babe, it's okay," I said and she rolled back over and drifted back to slumber. I crawled out of bed and headed for the bathroom. It appeared the Fish had their fun for the night, and they had indeed discovered my innermost fear!

Walking somberly into the bathroom, I glanced to the left and was startled by an image in my place in the huge mirror over the sink. I paused before the reflection in the dimly lit room,and pondered the visage before me, assisted only by illumination from a 7 watt night light in a wall socket.

Something is not right here. It is me....but....it's not me. Something is wrong. As I began to consider detail of the image before me, a conflict of reality subtley began to take place. The youthful, adventurous Rich known to my inner self seemed to be slowly evolving into a picture of an older, and more somber man with a furrowed brow, baggy, aging eyelids and crows feet at the temples. Hair all but gone from the top of the head....who the hell was this?

In my minds eye, images of a youthful Rich flashed through my mind; sunsets, sunrises, flying airplanes, fast boats and motorcycles, diving trips to the Carribean, tossing back a couple of ice cold brews.... party, party, party...inbetween periods of hard work, work, work...and always a couple more of those cold, cold, cold ones.....

Then the images began to change...to evolve magically as if first blurred by a cloak of mist and then clearing into a focused TV screen......First, the memories. Now the good remembrances were being folded into images of two failed marriages, the loneliness and guilt associated with those years of turmoil. Then momentary aftershocks of realizing those negative associations with people who had subtracted from the intended morals and values to be gained from life. The bad times were marching into my mind, taking over and overwhelming as if I had been stormed by a virtual army of negative thoughts.

As I struggled to extract myself from this imagery and confrontation with the recesses of my mind, I saw that the face in the mirror was now becoming more familiar. A recognizable, but unexpected, image materialized before my eyes as this tangled web of memories gradually released its assault on my mind. Memories of good, bad, confusing, and hazy recollections of a long ago father-son relationship that was less than perfect now began to roll through my mind like a bulldozer. My thoughts turned to images of my Dad's final days as he slowly slipped away from complications of lung cancer, no doubt induced by years of heavy smoking. The image in the mirror was clearly that of my father. And yet, it was me as well. Age and death had become two relevant subjects at the moment, thanks to this midnight message from your friendly "Fish Group."

"Sonofabitch," I muttered, as I snapped out of it, and staggered back to the bedroom. Approaching the king size bed, I paused for a long, hard, look at Mary and then crawled under the covers. I snuggled up close.... real close.....as I placed my head on her breast to sense her precious breathing and warmth, and then slowly drifted off to sleep.

The next night, I awoke, once more, to the inane raging of the aquarium babble. But, this time, instead of waiting for whatever death message they had planned for me, I enacted my newly formed "anti-Fish" plan. I had experienced my "limit" on the "not so funny" antics of the Fish!
"Fuck you!" I proclaimed, simultaneously lifting my head, grabbing my pillow, and then stuffing it over the top of my head and ears.

Mary, a sound sleeper, never stirred, and I wasn't long joining her. I felt liberated ! As far as I was concerned, the Fish would play their games without me from now on!

From that night forward, I'd like to say that they never came back...but that wasn't the case. The same ranting voice returned several times after that, but I just ignored it each time and rolled over and went back to sleep. Before long (2 or 3 weeks), that particular voice eventually stopped appearing. To this day, I will occasionally hear some conversation from the same aquarium source, but it seems to be of a different, not so radical, nature. I have decided to not do any recordings in the house so as to encourage the peace and sanctity of our home by simply not giving them a platform from which to speak.

Once in a while, while conducting an investigation, or on location and collecting EVP, I will obtain a message that seems ...well.. "rude," and in one case, I was notified by a considerate spirit to be careful, that the Fish were operating nearby. This humorous caution message from a friendly spirit on board the submarine USS Cavalla.

026- "Fish Talk....RUDE AGAIN....Don't bite!"

Is There No Privacy?

Privacy? It's all a figment of your imagination. Or a part of the reality that you construct for yourself. Or a part of the holographic universe which contains all that you are aware of, and all that you are not aware of as well. If you think you have privacy when you really need it, then that's about all you can hope for.....

When we study and experience the EVP phenomenon, we are quickly struck with the realization that we may at any time be visited, and even surrounded by a host of spiritual entities. Some of them may be deceased family members, or friends and aquaintances, or even strangers! Our human frailties easily cause us to rebel at this notion, and we become preoccupied with thoughts of indiscretions of our past that apparently were open to observation by all manner of spirits and beings! Can this really be?

Well, yes...and no. As it is with all things, there is considerably more to this issue than meets the eye of the earthbound spirit.

Believe me, spiritual entities in the astral planes are not as interested in your matters of privacy as you might think....However, If you have committed a crime, for instance...you better believe that the spiritual world knows.....They know all about it, and furthermore, they can be induced to make comments on the issue if approached properly. Of course, spirits may not have the option to make any of this information available to just anyone at any time and place. But my investigations frequently reveal cryptic and revealing comments from spirit voices that can incriminate an individual who has committed an immoral or harmful act towards others. These matters are not brought up unless humans are at the time focusing on those issues, and appear to be seeking a solution that will be of benefit to those concerned. Usually, there is not much concern for the perpetrator of the crime, as it would appear that it is their destiny to face the consequences of their actions.

When, on rare occasion, these types of incidents occur in the course of my studies and investigations, I frequently find myself slipping into a state of confusion and dis-orientation concerning what is reality and what is not. I am stonewalled by the revelation that these secrets and intimate bits of knowledge could be made available in any circumstance to an earth bound human. And indeed, it is fuel for many an argument and debate concerning the advisability of involving oneself in such matters while earthbound. In centuries long since past, people were burned at the stake for much less than this.I am certainly glad I am not living in an era with those sorts of beliefs.....

For those of us who live with the knowledge and true awareness of our spiritual existence, this issue has a reasonable explanation. Simply stated; if we are to accept the notion of survival of the spirit after death, then we must also accept the fact that our lives must have purpose. And that purpose would most likely be to gain spiritual knowledge from our earth experience and be able to apply those lessons learned to the benefit not only of mankind, but for the betterment of the spirit as well. So, it appears that for some of us, we can avail ourselves of tidbits of spiritual knowledge in order to further our purpose in our lives on earth. However, many others may never cross the path of the paranormal, as their intended purpose and spiritual goals on earth do not require assistance from spiritual knowledge at this time. It's just that simple, and I learned long ago that certain individuals will never accept one iota of spiritual information, no matter who is the bearer of that information or in what manner this information may be made available. That is meant to be, and may well be one of the reasons that knowledge of the paranormal remains reserved for select individuals whose spiritual purpose on earth requires it.

Based on that premise, we may always have the skeptics, the doubters, and the close minded. If our version of the spiritual reality is true, then we should celebrate that notion. It gives us purpose for being, and dignity to the existence of the uniqueness of each and every person on earth.

Now, regarding other more mundane matters of privacy....you know, like sex and such. It appears to me that spirits do not have much interest in violating a persons privacy, as in the case of a potential "peeping Tom." EVP spirits seem to enjoy speaking of "human desires and frailties" but it is not entirely clear to me what their purpose is.

For instance, many EVP researchers have noted considerable humor involved in statements by spiritual voices. But are their attempts at humor for their own benefit, or are these quips designed only to appeal to the humans interpreting the messages? Many researchers in related studies have noted that the spirit world may be in some cases more like earth than we might think. Robert A. Monroe, in his book "Journeys Out Of The Body" wrote that in astral travel experiences, it was common to feel sexual emotion and desire, and that spirits were inclined to live in communities that were inhabited by entities with similar likes and desires. So, perhaps, the spirit can indeed appreciate such things as sex, and humor, but for the most part, it is not possible to cross the dimensional line with those types of behavior.

I have known individuals who, in EVP sessions, have asked if any one was following them into the bathroom while they were taking a shower. The answers indicated that it was not a matter of interest that could pass through the spiritual barriers, and spirits almost never "spy" on those private moments. Nevertheless, make no mistake about it....If they want to tune into your bedroom momentarily to see who you are with....it is likely that if they have a good spiritual reason for doing so, indeed they will. However, adhering (hopefully) to a higher standard, they will make no judgements on what they observe, and undoubtedly the spirits have seen much....and told little.

The bottom line is that it's always been that way, so nothing has really changed except our own perception of the human ego. So now we are more humble in the knowledge that it is possible that we don't really have any secrets. Get used to it...it'll make you a better person. No more "airs" and all that....heh, heh

And, of course, in lighter moments the spirits really can come through with some choice comments. While I was doing an "undercover" EVP session in a hospital (using a hidden mike) I went to use the restroom while forgetting about the mike. As I unzipped, a female voice brightly exclaimed "Got One!"....Apparently spirits are not embarrassed easily, so relax. While on a field trip by myself in a rural cemetery, I had to relieve myself as a result of drinking too many soft drinks on the way over. As I stood by the fence, outside the cemetery, enjoying a moments relief................a female voice whispered clearly......

027- "He has to pee...now!"

That's right folks, there are times when there is no privacy, heh, heh....

Sex And The Paranormal

I have indulged in considerable "hand wringing" before coming to the public with this page. I was not sure if it would be appropriate, considering the many difficulties we in the "paranormal" biz experience with our public image and perception of what we do.

But after months of serious thought, it became more and more obvious that truth is always appropriate, and our sexuality is a certainly a large part of our lives and a major driving force behind our existence as human beings. Make no mistake about it, sex is a topic that spills over into the paranormal. It shows up in investigations and EVP recordings with regularity. And we get letters.........Boy, do we get letters...........

email:

"I have written to you previously about the ghost activity in my house. But now, something new has happened. It seems that something has been touching me at night. Sexually, I mean. Is this possible?"

Ann (Not real Name)

reply:

Dear Ann:

First, in answer to your direct question, yes, it is possible. However, let me state that these types of incidents rarely turn out to be caused by an entity, or ghost. There are many different causes for this type of incident that are not associated directly with ghost type behavior. Of course the most common would be "lucid dreaming." This can (and does) happen to all of us. Dreams frequently include some form of expressing sexual desire (and frustration as well), and may even result in orgasm on occasion. These dreams can seem extraordinarily real.

On the other hand, a very well known case involving a sexual attack on a female by a ghost was made into a movie. The authenticity of the incident is argued to this day, but one thing is for sure......the woman involved suffered serious mental anguish and torment because of the incidents.

From another perspective, Robert A. Monroe, author of "Journeys Out of the Body," writes in his books that sexual feelings are commonly felt and expressed in astral travel. One could conclude as well, that the spirit world, (at least in dimensions close to our world), may in fact retain some certain aspects of sexual attitudes, and is often quite obvious from spirit behavior.

When investigations lead too far into this sensitive area, I may prefer to call in a psychologist or family counselor for consultation. These issues can be quite complex.

RICH

email:
".....my boyfriend wanted to make love in a cemetery, and I wouldn't do it. It seemed disrespectful and I was basically afraid. He made fun of me and I wondered what you think about a ghost being upset over that....."

Meg (not real name)

reply:
Dear Meg:
Actually, I have a two part answer for you....one about your boyfriend, and one about the spiritual aspects of such an incident..

Regarding your boyfriend...his behavior seems selfish and somewhat immature. He needs to learn that a relationship requires respect for preferences of ones mate in sexual matters.

Discussion of the differences, not taunting, is the mature and meaningful manner of solving the issue. Our sexual preferences and desires can change and grow in many directions, given time. I suspect that you both are young, so tell your boyfriend to lighten up a bit and slow down. I suspect that he has a somewhat adventurous sexual nature, so why don't you have a discussion about his and your fantasies in that area, and proceed with something that will excite BOTH of you.

Now....As far as "upsetting" a ghost over a sexual encounter in a cemetery.....actually, I'm sure it's been done lots of times. The only thing I could say might be opinion gathered from the hundreds of spirits voices I have listened to from EVP gathered in cemeteries. Many voices seem to be carrying on conversation with each other. Others seem confused and call out to me for help. Still others have insisted that I leave! And most importantly, many others have graciously answered my questions and responded to my comments. This tells me that many are watching and listening to me.

For that specific reason, I would not care to participate in an encounter of that nature under those circumstances. It would be no different than going to a mall and trying that with a crowd of onlookers. Certainly, a diverse group of spirits would demonstrate all kinds of reactions,....some will protest...some might laugh...some might be deeply offended. After all, they are watching, and they are, or were, living people with feelings and opinions.

RICH

email:
Hey Rich;
"I was just wondering, do ghosts in your EVP use bad language or talk of sexual things...?"
LARRY

reply:
Hi Larry:

Quite frankly, the vast majority of EVP voices are well behaved when I am conducting field trips (Thank goodness LOL) This might be because I ask specific information from them and I am careful to eliminate any suggestion of hostility from my brief conversation. In investigations, however, many spirits may have an "axe to grind" and might spout off with unpredictable messages. I have heard some use foul language in a situation that seemed as though two spirits were at odds with each other. Then I have heard some just shout occasional expletives for reasons unknown to me. In these cases there was no difference in their outbursts and any other we might hear from a human encounter. I have also heard voices, female and male, using language to describe various portions of the human sexual anatomy, again for no apparent reason. These situations are all part of the mystery of the spirit world, and I am constantly amazed, stunned even,by these voices, especially when they talk right back to me immediately and answer a question I have just asked.

Oh yes, and here's an amazing thing...Never, not once (so far, knock on wood) has any spirit ever used suggestive or foul language to Mary. She has her own recorder for EVP, and I have mine. In fact, most spirits whisper when talking to Mary. It seems that her record is bound to fall at some point, but so far anyway this unusual showing of respect holds up. I suppose if we make a big thing of it, a spirit wise guy is bound to show up sooner or later though ! LOL

(UPDATE July 2003: Well, that expected "wise guy" showed up this summer. Mary had a rather vulgar and persistant spirit follow her around in the hill country. While chanting about his lurid desires, a friendly spirit guide came in and warned him off...)

Maybe, just maybe, I will put together a CD with all the voices I cannot put up on the internet. But I am still considering the spiritual ramifications of publishing anything and everything I receive. It could just be that some of these messages were not meant for me to publish. I will have to think and rethink on this for awhile

RICH

Lonestar Flight Museum

I live in a neighborhood, not far from Scott Field in Galveston, Texas, where it is not unusual to hear a loud engine noise coming from above you, and then find yourself looking into the sky at what seems for all the world to be a true "rip in the fabric of space and time". From behind a cloud will magically appear, in all its glory, an authentic WW ll B-17 bomber, or even a couple of original Japanese Zeros storming noisily through the heavens above you ! The sight and sound spectacle of these aircraft are as "out of this world" as a UFO sighting !

These rare vintage aircraft have been painstakingly and impeccably restored and brought back to life by a group of highly dedicated airmen, making their base of operations now at the Galveston air strip, and housing their works of art at the Lonestar Flight Museum. The degree of attention to detail, craftsmanship, and untold hours of toil, have made these extraordinary aircraft difficult to describe in words. Pictures do little justice to the reality of standing in their presence.

Indeed, there is about these craft an aura of unmistakable historical dignity, and the surrounding atmosphere is supercharged with emotion. While standing near these magnificent machines, it is impossible to not plunge oneself into a world of wonderment, while pondering the profound changes thrust upon the lives of the crews and their families as a result of these planes' combat missions in the most horrific war mankind has ever known.

The thought had often occurred to me that anyone who had strong worldly ties to military aviation, (and these types of vintage aircraft in particular), may have a reason to visit these craft after having passed from the earth and into the spirit world. In fact, it seemed to me that vast numbers of spirits could be lurking in the shadows of these craft for any number of reasons, and as I have a similar interest and military background in aviation, I could not resist an investigation of the premises.

It is my usual practice to try to select visitation times in public places to be in the "off" hours, so I chose to head out at the earliest permissible time of the morning. Tourists are not usually fond of getting an early start, and I hoped to find the crowd minimal, so as to not cause a lot of extra interference from chatting visitors while I operated my digital recorders.

This trip would be on a week end and close to home, but unfortunately on this day Mary was not feeling well. During most of our EVP and paranormal work, we would normally not bring along our youngsters, but this day I would find myself with our two teenagers off school for the day, and of course quite reluctant to miss out on this opportunity to visit the museum.

There are valid reasons to be cautious of exposing young children to paranormal phenomena. In some cases, adult situations and language may occur. Certain incidents may not be understood by children, and could create unwarranted fears about the meaning of their observations.. Of course, younger children can also contribute to a disorderly atmosphere that may not be favorable specifically to conducting EVP recordings...everything from too much noise and conversation, to the very real fact that children can themselves add unknowingly to a general psychic disruption of paranormal phenomena. Children commonly have strong psychic abilities and can manifest without being aware of what they do.

In this case, our teen son and daughter, aged 16 and 15, are no strangers to the paranormal, and are quite well behaved....(except for that "sibling rivalry" thing....jeeez). Oh well, all things considered, I was glad to be able to spend the time with them and I knew they would enjoy the museum. Maybe their busy teen age minds and hormones would stir up some interesting ghostly comments. We all began to look forward to the outing.

As we drove up to the entrance of the museum, we were struck by the size of the huge hangar and upon entering found there were two main showroom areas. Numerous aircraft of all kinds and description, as well as many other items such as aviation support equipment, missiles, gun turrets, and even antique vehicles of the era such as autos and motorcycles were on display. The ceilings were extremely high, and it seemed that a football game, with audience, could easily be played in each section of the massive hangar. A third area, with lower ceiling and smaller exhibits of items such as uniforms, medals, models, photos, memorabilia, and displays with stories about the planes, their crews, and the war in general, was located off to one side.

On my only previous visit, several years ago, they had aircraft parked outside the hangars, and it was possible on that occasion to go inside some of those planes. Unfortunately on this day, we found the outside aircraft had been deployed to an airshow at another city, so we were just out of luck. I asked if any management/staff was there and the young person at the desk replied they were all at the show . I was somewhat dissapointed as I had wanted to get one of the staff to allow me inside some of the aircraft for photos and EVP, but now I would have to be happy with the "tourist" view for this visit.

Well, I'll make the best of it then, I thought...and as I surveyed the hangar and took in the atmosphere surrounding these fine aircraft, I had no doubt that spirits were not only close by, but already speaking to us. I quickly turned on my recording apparatus, and we began touring the monstrous rooms as I mentally projected my thoughts outward to the spirit world in existence all around us....

The Spirits come forth.......

It was time to get down to business...As the kids shuffled onward and a ways ahead of me, I began to fall back a bit in order to gain a little space of my own. Surveying the immediate surrounding area, and finding myself somewhat isolated in a section of the museum, I began to speak softly ....

"Hello...if there are any spirits who can see or hear me now, I am seeking communication with those spirits who have passed on from their lives on earth. We are at this Lonestar Museum today and looking at all these fine old aircraft. We would love to hear any messages that any spirits may have to say about these elegant aircraft."

The reaction from the spirit world was immediate, and it appeared that we had attracted the attention of at least one ghostly presence, as a solitary, and very supportive female voice came forward and boldly issued a challenge..... "Magnificent.....she stated, "Prove it....you're up !"

028- "Magnificent.... prove it, you're up"

Things were certainly off to a great start, and as I meandered between the shiny metallic pieces of history, I snapped photos left and right, eager to make a permanent record of the displays. Our early hour of arrival had worked well for us also, as there were only a handful of people in the entire museum. At the moment, no one at all was in sight except for the kids who were now strolling back in my direction.

We joined up, and then walked together for a while, discussing our various impressions and feelings that had been conjured by the magic of the surreal display of aircraft from the past.

As we walked and talked, unknown to us our recorders were tracking the activities of some special guests ! Apparently, the teens had summoned forth a spirit crowd of their own, as younger voices began to show up in our presence.The first young voice seemed interested in commenting on my picture taking, and due to our own conversation, I was only able to isolate a portion of his comment, although it was an appropriate one.. "Every single picture taken"....he mused, and then paused with a typical teenaged "ummmm....".Unfortunately, our chatter covered the rest of his statement, but we were pleased to note that the kids had some peer group attention from the spirit world on this outing.

029- "Every single picture taken.......ummm..."

The younger spirit generation seemed to follow the kids throughout our visit this day, and as we detoured into the adjoining display room which contained smaller exhibits, we again found an astounding snippet of conversation between two younger male spirits. One, who was referred to as "Eddie", seemed to be a "lesser experienced" version of a ghost, and his friend seemed to be engaged in some helpful explanation in the differences in our perception of reality and theirs. Eddie spoke first as he voiced his fears of being recognized by us mortals."They already see me ! "whereupon Eddie's friend reminds him..."Eddie, you don't gotta talk !"

030- "They already see me"... "Eddie, you don't gotta talk !"

Spirits appear from everywhere !

While we were in the exhibit area of the Lonestar Flight Museum, I decided to slip away for a moment as I am accustomed to doing in all my investigations in electronics voice phenomena. As it had turned out, many spirits so far had apparently been attracted to the youngsters accompanying me, and had thus far appeared in a young version of spirit form as well. As I distanced myself slightly from the children once more, I wondered if then my ghostly audience would return to a more mature appearance.

I slipped through the doorway, and back into the hangar amongst the aircraft. There was a stillness about the huge room, and tourists were few, and far between. I took this quick moment to restate my request to the spirit world...

"Any spirits who can see or hear me now, as I walk among these old aircraft, please speak....I would like to hear your voice." I respectfully spoke these words into the reality of my world, all the while concentrating on the fact that my inner self provided me comforting knowledge that I was not alone here....

Hear Rich's voice recorded as he actually speaks to the spirit world in the museum....

031- "Any spirits who can see or hear me now....."

And the reply, in mere seconds, came from a cheerful female voice with only a brief, but to the point.... "HI !"...

032- "Hi !"

After this point, I began to pick up EVP at a much faster pace. Quickly, I received two very unusual messages, which sounded as if they were whispered, or perhaps required some source of noise as a carrier which caused them to appear as a wispy or whispering sound. Normally, these kinds of EVP wind up on the "cutting room floor" as they may be difficult for the inexperienced ear to discern. But in this case, these messages were quite in context with the theme of the aircraft museum, and I thought it important that you all be given a shot at letting your ear bring you what possibly may be actual aircraft voice transmissions of the past....Listen carefully in quiet surroundings, and repeat the message to yourself as you listen to these actual spirit voices.........

033- "Report....landing gear..."

034- "man...lookit man...do not pull up !"

At this point, voices began to fill every available space on the recordings. Many were overlapping, and others would talk over our own conversations and occasional noise from inside the museum. From within the hangar came a steady, but low din of 40's style music playing from some unseen device. On occasion, the music could be faintly heard in the background of the ghostly voice recordings, adding considerably to the surrealistic mood of the moment. In some instances, the ghost voices appeared to take on the tempo of the music, somehow even managing at times to follow the exact cadence of the songs...yet each and every voice had it's own unique message, it's own identifiable timbre and masculine or feminine gender, all of which is typical of the wonder of the EVP mystery.

above: photo shows gun turrets aft and on the side of this WW II aircraft

Excerpts of a ghostly military briefing !......

The following sequence of recorded voices from the Lonestar Flight Museum may well be considered by some readers to be one of *most unusual* demonstrations of EVP collected on this date.

The following half dozen EVP recordings appear to contain segments of conversation that could represent portions of a military briefing. It is next to impossible to determine the total meaning of all these messages as they are not recorded in their entirety, but rather in collections of brief phrases.these phrases make sense in their own partiality, but leave us in the dark as to the complete meaning of the entire "briefing."

Try to imagine a scenario of a meeting of military men, some of whom may be pilots, as they use the following phrases in a discussion of strategy or military importance. Some remarks contain unique terms which may be personal in nature, but still related to the military topic at hand......

035- "Navy rules I grew up with...."

036- "the next battle sequence..."

037- "the lack of physical key solution..." (OK, here's one for you to fret over ! We listened to this one over and over, and each time it seemed to say something different. We were sure it belonged in this group with the other "briefing" dialogue, but no one can yet agree on what the fellow is saying...have fun ! Rich)

038- "Gralum, repeat the reposition..."   (Gralum...someone's name ??)

039- "usually I pick 'em....today is the one...."

above: photo shows P-38 lightning with many Trophy marks beneath the cockpit

This one with an unusual twist......it uses a term which is more representative of slang in the 40's, than nowadays. Perhaps we might hear this in a rare instance, but chances are it would be an "old timer" who was saying it....

040- "No Siree....Duke !"

Above: These are a collection of medals won by a P38 pilot. No doubt there are many stories untold of human drama, emotion, and heroism concerning the history of these craft and their crews.

Perhaps some of these EVP messages are an attempt to bring these stories to light...

The next message from beyond was an extraordinarily clear phrase, but with perhaps a meaning only known by the entity who expressed these sentiments...."Let her do good motion..." said a male voice while I snapped my photos of the above aircraft......

041- "Let her do good motion..."

What do you think he meant ?

"Confused and Lost" Souls

In almost every EVP study I do, I find a few comments by some entities that reveal themselves as "lost" souls, or at least as spirits who may not have settled on a satisfactory direction towards becoming one with God. I have come to realize that this may be as natural as it is for us humans to stray momentarily from our intended moral and spiritual paths here on earth. I can assure you that my years of study in this field all point to an eventual recovery for these confused spirits, and my personal research shows corroboration and agreement by most all psychics and experiencers of OBE's and NDE's in this regard.

The following EVP message recorded at the Lonestar Museum is somewhat typical of those few straying spirits who show up on all recording sessions......

042- "Let go of me ....sweet Jesus help.."

This had been an enjoyable and informative visit. The kids loved it, and the EVP recordings were astonishing. This had, in fact, been my first attempt to locate spirits in a museum, and now as I began to appreciate the spirit world's interest in this historical building and its treasures, I decided to make a note to search for more interesting museums to visit in the future.

As we strolled through the souvenir store and towards the exit, I wondered what would make a good finale to our adventure for the day....As usual, a spirit voice came to the rescue, and with extraordinarily few words, gave us our cue......

043- "That's done it !..." was the short and sweet message.

"Yes sireee, duke...!" I smiled....." I do believe that's about done it"

Fredericksburg, Texas

In the heart of the Texas Hill Country, Fredericksburg has always been a favorite spot of ours to visit. Our kids go to summer camp near Kerrville, and we pass through Fredericksburg every year on the way to their camp. It is not possible to drive through the quaint town without stopping! Be sure to bring cash and charge cards though, as their shops offer a wonderful selection of unique, quality products and gifts. The people are friendly, the restaurants are great, and the historical atmosphere is evident everywhere.

Fredericksburg was founded by a handful of German immigrants in 1845. The settlers were beset by hardships that must have been impossible for us to imagine in our present state of society, and the lifespan was short indeed, due mostly to plagues of disease that ran rampant through the territory.

This would be a fine place to search for ghostly spirits ! We would spend time here both on the way down to Kerrville, and on the way back as well. A little prior research had set our goals for investigation at four locations near our scenic hill country destination..

1. *Der Staht Cemetery* - prairie burial place of many pioneers of long ago
2. *The old Fredericksburg Jailhouse* - a surprisingly active spot for spirits!!
3. *Fort Martin Scott* - a small collection of ruins of an old military outpost
4. *Enchanted Rock* - a huge granite dome, long ago revered by Indians for strange noises and lights emanating from the rock at night.

We rolled into Fredericksburg on the 30th of May and got right down to business. No shopping this time, all our time would be devoted to making new acquaintances with "old" residents of Fredericksburg!

Der Stadt Friedhof

The first thing we saw as we approached the entrance to the Fredericksburg German Cemetery was a huge ornate wrought Iron Gate, semi circular across the top with the name "Der Stadt Friedhof." No doubt we were at the right place. Gazing across the small prairie, we detected a subtle, but distinctive design to the layout and construction of the graves.

Although through the years a randomness to the placement of graves had occurred, many of the graves employed some type of rustic decorative iron fencing, creating an atmosphere of privacy and unique separation to each site. Another common mode of construction for the grave sites included a small curb like wall around the perimeter of the site. Most of these curbed-in enclosures had a layer of gravel spread evenly across the interior. In some cases, ornaments such as figurines, shells, and small toys could be found on the gravel inside the protective walls.

There was an unusual stillness in this arid prairie like existence, and a stark contrast from the hustle and bustle of the downtown tourist laden Fredericksburg of the 21st century. Prickly pear cactus fared well here and there about the graveyard, but there was little evidence of any other green plants in the current 100+ degree dry summer heat. The burial ground was scenic, in an "old west" sort of way, but one couldn't help but sense feelings of despair and sadness. Later, when we looked closely at the early history of this pioneer community, it became obvious that hardship and misery was indeed the order of the day. Our overwhelming sense of concern for the human spirits interred here was justified.

"AMERICA, a free earth, among a people free" was the popular cry in Germany, where more than 50 books on America were published in Germany between 1815 and 1850.

"TEXAS, A great golden land" was the further cry of many of those writers who helped start the movement from the politically torn Germany to the new promised land. A surge of immigration into Texas was also created by the Revolution of 1848, an abortive attempt to unify the German government. Leaders of the liberal movement, the so-called "Forty-Eighters," came to Texas because of persecution at home for their roles in the revolution.

The promise made in Germany was, to each man who was 21 years of age, a half-acre town lot and 10 acres in the countryside to those brave enough to settle the new Texas territories.

It took the first German colonists about three months to sail across the Atlantic and through the Gulf of Mexico, making landfall at Indianola on the Texas Gulf coast. On the old sailing ships life was hard. Jerky and hardtack were the only foods, and vegetables or fruit were not available.Scurvy, dysentery, and cholera took their toll on the settlers as their situation became worse from malnutrition. Many who made it to Indianola in 1845 contracted malaria from mosquitoes and died.

The Germans began a long difficult trek across the state without resources, adequate transportation, or supplies, and many suffered from disease and died along the way. Others dropped out and settled where they could. Communities were established all along a wide corridor leading from the coast to Central Texas, as well as in other areas of the state.

Fredericksburg was first occupied on May 8, 1846, by about 120 settlers after a two-week trip from New Braunfels. Sixteen ox-drawn wagons, protected from Indian attack by mounted guards, carried the settlers. The following year the Anglo establishment was astonished by an honored peace treaty with the Comanches that was orchestrated by the Germans and their community leaders.

By 1900, Texas was home to an estimated 150,000 ethnic Germans. The Fredericksburg and hill country area was shaped by German culture and history, and made valued contributions to Texas in the fields of history, literature, agriculture, food, architecture, music and art.

But those great contributions were not without sacrifice. Building homes, businesses, and an entire city from the ground up was a monumental task.cholera epidemics swept across the state, often taking the greater part of entire families to their graves. Estimates are that half, or more, of these settlers lost their lives before achieving their goals in the settling of this territory.

And here we stood on this hallowed burial ground, face to face with the evidence of their massive human pain and suffering.

We could feel it. The air was heavy with emotion, and we knew very well that we were surrounded by spirits who had carried extreme karmic burdens during their short lives.

We would try to communicate with them.....but, what would we say? How could we not feel guilt for simply just being here with our many comforts and conveniences? I was not sure I would feel worthy spiritually.

I decided to just turn on the recorders, and begin slowly, without speaking and let the words find the way to me. Mary and Jennie headed off in one direction with one recorder, and I in the other.

The spirits are watching, and talking!

I had only just set up Mary's digital recorder, and sent her on her way, when after only 2 seconds, a woman's voice came sharply through with a surprising message...

"You take a gun!"... admonished the motherly like voice.

Wow....it seemed we were off to a rather interesting start to say the least. But then, considering we were in the midst of pioneer spirits who had passed on while fighting all types of adversity, I suppose advising someone to "take a gun" would not be at all unusual.

044- "You take a gun!"

As Mary and our teen daughter continued on their pathway through the cemetery, they chatted as they walked. In fact, they chatted a bit too much. As it is our usual practice to to undergo these types of investigations with a minimum of people (usually just Mary and I) they had forgotten the rules..keep talking to a minimum! As a result, it appears the spirits were more interested in listening to Mary and Jennie talk, then they were in talking to them.

On several occasions, spirits were interrupted by the conversation, but as always, we did manage to get a few more significant EVP samples from her digital.

On one brief quiet spell, a voice whispered emphatically "Preacher", but we are pretty much without any other spirit conversation to go along with this and further describe the context of the message.

045- "Preacher"

At a random moment in the meandering of the two, a male voice suddenly popped up and shouted "HEY !"

No telling what that was about.....but the shout was just as clear as if a strange man had been standing right beside them...

046- "HEY!"

Our stroll through the cemetery took about 15 minutes. During that time with the girls talking, and a slow moving but noisy airplane contributing to a noisy background, we subsequently did not obtain not many EVP on the girls recorders.Their recordings did contain some German words which were not suitable audio quality for the book CD, but which were audible to us on our analyzing equipment. We know nothing of the German language, but most seemed to contain names of people.

Meanwhile, I was on a separate path, quite by myself, and managed to at least keep quiet surroundings for the recorder.

I managed to pick up a few very interesting characters on the recorder. The first voice I picked up was indeed not German, but nevertheless a family type message ...."mamas kidding me...papa."

047- "mamas kidding me...papa"

Many who study EVP find that received messages may be in our own native tongue even though we may even be in a foreign country. It is not known why this occurs, but it is theorized that a spirit may communicate any way they wish. Perhaps that is true, but I have also obtained foreign phrases in foreign areas as well. (Particularly in cemeteries of a particular majority ethnic population.) On this day, indeed the majority of the phrases we recorded were in English, and the few German ones were weak and difficult to discern.

In this unique message "Donald, take (more?) and find her", it appears that perhaps a father or grandfather was trying to advise someone on pursuing a lost love perhaps? I hope Donald understands this, I don't!!

048- "Donald, take (more) and find her"

Mary's name comes up once again in an EVP, as a raspy spirit voice simply states "Mary....beyond" Of course Mary was a popular name then and now, so we don't know if this was directed at Mary in this particular instance. However, we have recorded our names in reply to our requests many times...

049- "Mary....beyond"

A REMINDER

By the way, let me remind you all just one more time to always make sure you are listening to your EVP CD under optimum listening conditions. Because these voices cannot be heard by the ear most of the time, we must employ the use of extensive technology to amplify and bring up the voices from static and noise levels within the recordings so we can hear them. They will not be perfect because they are not voices! They are voice patterns derived from magnetic field disturbances noted in the surroundings of our activities. Always use good equipment to listen, and repeat the EVP many times over. You will find that your ear will soon get accustomed to picking out the voices and the more you listen, the more you will hear!

This final EVP from the Fredericksburg Cemetery will remain a mystery as to its meaning. A man shouts an encouraging "Go get him, PoPo!" I suppose PoPo could be a nickname, an Indian, or even someone's dog. Your guess is as good as mine!

050- "Go get him, PoPo !"

The three of us had toured the small burial area now, and we finished by passing through the children's graves. The Germans apparently buried their children all in rows in one section of the graveyard, supposedly to allow them to play together in the afterlife. We did not pick up anything in the way of EVP here, but we certainly picked up a huge degree of sadness at the rows and rows of very young children, many showing their death date the same as their birth date. No doubt the terrible scourge of cholera had taken a heavy toll on these people.

The temperature today was already 101 degrees in Fredericksburg and it was barely noon. We had heard about a jailhouse in town dating from the mid 1800's, so we packed 'em up and headed off to the Chamber of Commerce to get directions. The air conditioning in the car felt good, but again I felt guilty until I was out of sight of the spirit folks at Der Stadt Cemetery.....All the hard work and suffering they put out in their short lives, and here they stay while we drive off in air conditioning to get a double cheeseburger and have a good time. I hope some of them got to come back in a later life to enjoy this great little town in its prime.

The Old Fredericksburg Jail

After leaving the old German Cemetery, we cruised by the local Chamber of Commerce office to get some info about the old jail someone had told us about. The Chamber office had moved, so we followed directions (posted on the window)to the new building which was just around the corner. We received a very courteous welcome, but was told that the jail was not open to the public. They did have a special function once a year when the building was open for a tour, but that was it.

This was not necessarily good news. However, there was a brighter side to it. For one thing, we actually don't always need to be inside a building to contact spirits within. We have found that spiritual presence is usually aware of our needs to communicate without respect to earthly physical distance. In fact, I have received messages from the same spirit in different locations hundreds of miles away from the last location of EVP. So, we would got to the jail anyway, and see if we could approach the building from the outside. Another good thing is that if the place was not open to the public, we would have the grounds to ourselves, and spirits would give us their undivided attention.

Arriving at the jail, we were treated to a most impressive sight. The old building was in remarkable condition, built of large stone blocks, and with doors and windows covered with a massive web of steel bars. The windows were tall and narrow, and it was obvious that absolutely no one was going to escape from this building, at least not through those windows ! Surrounding the building was a tall stone wall with wrought iron on the top and across the street side front of the jail the iron fence added an old fashioned, but decorative touch. The building itself was not large, but seemed to be very tall for the two story design. It would appear from the outside that it would have very high ceilings.

What little information we had, informed us that a living quarters on the first floor was provided for the caretaker, or jailman. On the upper floor, were two separate areas, one for normal containment, and another to house high security risk prisoners. The bars on the top floor windows were definitely larger and stronger looking on two of those windows, which must have indicated the security cells.

Not a soul in sight, we had the whole place to ourselves. The front gate was invitingly unlocked, and I strolled through the gate and began to walk the perimeter of the foreboding jail building. Standing up next to the structure, it was even more apparent how unusually tall it was for just a two story building.

I stopped in the rear doorway, and spoke out loud to the spirit inhabitants of this historical site, dating back to the mid 1800's. "Hello, my name is Richard, and I am seeking communication with spirits. I seek to hear the voices of those who have passed on from their lives on earth. If you can see or hear me now, please speak and I will be able to hear your voice from the recording devices I am using here"

As it would turn out, there was almost no need to go into the building to contact the spirits. I was barraged by a number of voices, so many in fact that it was unusually difficult to separate them.

I was asked for help by no less than two entities, who simply asked "Help me." Here is one of the two voices...

051- "Help me!"

In another mix of two voices, a male voice loudly states "Jailkeeper," while a female voice in the background simultaneously says "can't believe you said that"

052- "Jailkeeper"

I peeked through two downstairs windows at the rear of the jailhouse, and was able to see (through hazy glass panes) that the room was obviously the jailhouse living quarters, and was complete with antique furnishings of the period. This certainly was an appealing target for an indoor study, and I made a mental note to contact the city fathers on my next trip to see if I could gain entrance. No telling if these hill country folk would "cotton to a city slicker snooping around lookin' for ghosts and such", but I must give it a try anyway.

My next EVP message was an eerie cry from a youngster. Sounds like a little boy, asking "Where's Mikey?" I have on many occasions, at different locations around Texas, recorded a very similar voice of a youngster, In addition, I have a few samples of his voice on my web site, and that single EVP message has attracted more attention from readers than any other. People have written me from around the world to tell me that they were profoundly moved in some way upon hearing this particular voice. We all have a soft spot for children, and perhaps this voice is just playing on our own vulnerability, but there have been many times when these voices have hit Mary and I in a weak spot. We are frequently driven to great depths of meditation upon realizing the reality of truth and relevance in some of the messages.

053- *"Where's Mikey?"*
Jailhouse Booty?

The next EVP messages will get your imagination going for sure!

An authoritative male voice started it all by exclaiming "Near the rock, soldier!" Then another voice chimed in.. "That's worth...millions!"

Obviously there could be problems here in translating the exact meaning of these somewhat ambiguous statements from the spirit world. Now I don't want to cause a stampede of treasure hunters or anything, because these EVP voices could have been referring to almost anything in a previous or even a future investigation, but it certainly gives reason to pause for further examination! The most astounding issue related to these EVP are that references to Spanish gold and silver treasure in the hill country are quite common historically in literature and legend. And would you believe that one of the most famous in this area is the "Enchanted Rock," otherwise commonly referred to as "the Rock" and mentioned not once, but twice in a meaningful manner in these spirit comments! After this, we were looking forward to visiting the Enchanted Rock!

054- *"Near the rock, soldier!"*

055- *"That's worth...millions!"*

Then the next message, also including a reference to the "Rock", is telling me to "not leave 'lieben' .....where the rock shows." "Lieben" is a German term of endearment meaning "love" or "honey or sweetheart;" (At this point I was not sure how to take this message, although on the following days trip to the

Enchanted Rock, it became crystal clear that this was a prophetic warning to not leave Mary alone while at the rock! Driving the winding country roads towards the Enchanted Rock, we suddenly came over a hill and were afforded a wonderful view of a wide expanse of valley, from which rose majestically a huge rock dome.the words of the spirit voice were now the focus of our attention....what would this warning mean? and why was it given to us from the jailhouse?)

056- "Do not leave Lieben, where the rock shows"

During our brief visit to the old jail, Mary and Jennie had stayed in the car, waiting to see first what kind of success I had. As I rounded the building about 10 minutes later, they both got out and came on to the jailhouse grounds to get an "up close" look.

At this time, Jennie received her first official notice from the spirit world, as I recorded the voice saying "Here...Jennie" followed by a "PS...I love ya!"

057- "Here Jennie"

058- "PS...I love ya"

Jennie, who is going on 16 years old, had never been with us on an EVP trip before. We have previously been somewhat protective of the kids in this respect, although, truth is, to this date we have no real reason to fear anything from EVP. In fact, most of our experiences have yielded benign messages. To be sure, some of them have been "X-rated", but these events always occur when in context with the interest in subjects instigated by me. For instance, in "Spirits in the Hood" as I announced my intentions to interview street people and prostitutes, I was immediately flooded with exuberant characters with many sexual expletives and language during that adventure. Likewise, when in circumstance that demands proper behavior, the spirits seem to adhere to the standards set by my needs. Most of the time, that is.

We had told Jennie that a spirit had spoken her name, and she seemed quite surprised, but a little unsure. She did not request immediately to listen, but eventually the curiosity got to her. Truth is, when she first heard the voices, she said "that's creepy." but after hearing the follow-up "PS, I love ya" she smiled and registered   astonishment at the personal and affectionate message. "That's cool," she beamed, and I believe a major barrier had just been removed from her mind. She would most likely look forward to future EVP sessions.But you can be sure Mary and I will always carefully evaluate all EVP before presenting them to the kids.

For our final EVP of the jailhouse session, we picked up a soul who seemed to have a need to be philosophical about love. Of course, in EVP, the majority of references to love I think probably refer to "spiritual love" the essence and purpose for our being. Perhaps the way this fellow stated it, it applies to life and death as well..... "It hurts givin' love..."

059- "It hurts giving love..."

On that somber note, we once again jumped into our faithful Toyota, cranked up the A/C, and headed out to our next adventure. Before heading off to the Enchanted Rock, we planned to stop by and visit the ruins of old Fort Martin Scott, at the edge of town. Perhaps we could rustle up some old soldiers for a conversation!

Fort Martin Scott

stockade-ghost face above door   *closer view- face of ghost*

First impressions can be wrong, I guess. Our first look at this small group of buildings gave us the feeling that there might not be too much paranormal activity at this spot. The history of the old Fort tells us that it was active only from 1848 to 1853, and was primarily a housing, training and supply post.

However, for the next 106 years, the fort was occasionally used by Texas Rangers, soldiers of the Confederacy, various homesteaders, and finally ownership by the Braeutigam family which owned the 640 acres for 89 years. In this case, we should have considered that there is no way for us to really tell what kind of spiritual activity might be in a specific locale until we open ourselves to communication with the spirit world. In fact, this tiny little patch of history turned out to be a very active source of EVP, as well as the home of a "jail bound" spirit who produced his image for us in a stockade photo!

The rest of the family had expressed a desire to do some shopping, and I seized upon the opportunity to drop them all off at a nearby store while I scouted the old fort by myself. This way I could avoid any possibility of conflicts with too much family chatter while trying to capture EVP.

Only one vehicle in the Fort Martin Scott parking lot...that was great. I should have most of the place to myself, which is the way I prefer. I stopped by the office entrance, and found that admission is free. Some artifacts (soldier uniforms, swords etc) were on display in the lobby, and maps, models, and pictures added a little historical perspective. It was a modest layout so far, but what the heck. I have found ghosts standing on streetcorners before, so I knew there would be something here for me to contact.

The gentleman at the office explained that all buildings on the grounds were duplications of old drawings, maps and pictures. Except for one. Ah, yes. except for just one single building, and that one, the old stockade, was still preserved in pretty much its original state with a few repairs. This was good news, as a stockade, or jailhouse, usually contains an atmosphere of emotion and frequently is a "hot spot" for ghostly activity. I headed right to the old stockade without hesitation.

This was a small building, containing two large rooms with a huge wooden door and a bulky steel latch. Adjoining one room was another thick door with steel latch and bars which led to a hallway and entrance to 4 individual cells. These cells were very narrow (approx 4 feet wide) and about 8 to 10 feet long. The ceiling was high, and had a very narrow slit in the wall up high on the roof to allow some light into each cell from outside.

I started my digital recording apparatus, and began to take a few photos. Moments later, while reviewing the pictures I had taken, I was astonished to find a ghostly apparition above one of the cell doors! An image of the upper body, shoulders, and head of an older man with bushy hair and beard, and a neckerchief around his neck was clearly visible. This would be the only ghostly apparition captured by us on this days outing, but that was certainly sufficient. Good ghost photos are difficult to come by, especially in the daytime!

Excited by this development, I concentrated on photos and recordings, stopping frequently to speak out loud to any spirits that might be listening. Good thing no one else was around. It had taken me a long time to get comfortable with talking out loud to spirits, especially in a public place! (No doubt a fella could get some odd stares that way...) But now this was old hat to me and I moved around the property and tried to imagine what the old fort would have been like when it was fully occupied by soldiers.

I stepped outside behind the stockade and found two huge, very old oak trees, behind which ran a clear rock bottom stream. Up hill on the other side of the stream was a vast prairie and on the other side of the prairie, a wooded area. In the midst of the prairie was a single deer, grazing comfortably in the afternoon sun. No wonder the Braeutigam family held on to this land for 89 years. I found it remarkable that I found myself here on this day to enjoy such a scene. It is so difficult these days to find any place close to nature without spoilage by mans presence. (In fact, I read recently that explorers now are trying to close off Mt Everest to climbing, as so many people are climbing up the peak now, that much of their time is spent cleaning up litter ! sheez, don't get me started!)

SPIRITS BREAK THEIR SILENCE

Moving back into the stockade area, voices began to take note of my presence and make comments.The first to speak was a voice which demanded to "Lock the door" followed by a "thump" which for all intents and purposes must be assumed to be one of those huge wooden doors slamming. A most remarkable EVP. As usual, I heard nothing while in the stockade.

060- "Lock the door"..... "thump"

Then, a plaintive plea from a male voice who registered genuine distress, as he stated "Don't... like... them"... " Help me"

061- "Don't....like....them"..... "Help me"

Then a most interesting comment from yet another voice that I must assume was a prisoner. In this EVP you will actually hear my voice within a cell in the stockade, as I ask for comments. The reply is "He beat me."

062- "He beat me"

All of the previous EVP messages were recorded in or near the vicinity of the old stockade and I couldn't help but wonder if the apparition in the stockade belonged to any of the voices in the recordings.

I followed the path from the stockade and walked back towards the street and office. On my right was a row of living quarters for soldiers. The first building was only a rock foundation, and nothing else was there. I stopped and sat on the rocks, and spoke out loud requesting any soldiers who had actually been here at this old fort during it's operation to please speak to me. I was again astounded to find that I had recorded a voice which purported to be a Colonel in the Cavalry! "Cavalry...Colonel Bartlett"

063- "Cavalry...Colonel Bartlett"

Later, I dug through some old records, and was not able to find a Col. Bartlett attached directly to Fort Scott. However, that doesn't mean it didn't occur as records from that era are difficult to authenticate. I did find several Col. Bartletts, however, in various positions of service during those years that could have come through the fort, or could have been attached temporarily in some manner. Many temporary occupations of this fort were known to have occurred by confederate and other troups.

While strolling through the officers quarters and in and around the foundations of these old buildings, I captured the following interesting comments....

064- "Anna" - I assume the wife or lover of a soldier?

065- "Hot Toddy"- a popular elixir usually of a homemade recipe which includes a shot of whiskey

066- "He helped make it good, Billy"- Your guess is as good as mine....

067- "OK, wife is pregnant"- This from within a building for officers known to have wives living in........

068- "Old Spike....whoop" - This is one of the more unusual EVP of the entire group. We have all registered guesses as to the meaning of this statement...one suggestion was that a person stepped on a spike, and let out a whoop! Another was that "Old Spike" was just a character, and the whoop was to imply he was a humerous person.

Although my first impression was that this would be a modest paranormal experience, needless to say, I was wrong. The EVP and the photo were of exceptional quality. In fact, I was pleased indeed to have a repeat performance of the spirit comment phenomenon which frequently gives me a cue to end the segment I am researching. Just as I was searching for a wrap-up to the old fort trip, here a spirit voice signs me off...... "That is all...son"

069- "That is all...son"

"Yep, on that note, I reckon, that will be all for now, ..."

Enchanted Rock
A PORTAL FOR SPIRITUAL ACTIVITY

Our next stop in the west Texas Hill Country was the legendary huge natural granite dome, Enchanted Rock, known historically for it's Indian and pioneer lore. The tales date back to Spanish explorers, Indians and pioneers settling the area, and reputed treasures of gold and silver hoarded in secret mines in this very location and nearby. As the story goes, the 640 acre, nearly 400 foot high dome received it's name from Indian reports of spirit lights and night time noises emanating from the giant rock. The Indians had great respect for the huge natural monument, and some would not set foot upon it. Others used it for ceremony or observation and there were some beliefs that human sacrifice had taken place at the site.

We are tempted to chalk up the origin of the spirit light tales to superstition, except for the fact that while we were there, we did indeed photograph a mysterious moving bright blue sphere, in bright daylight, which appeared in two successive photos about 30 seconds apart. And the most incredible assortment of recorded ghostly voices we have ever encountered took us weeks to sort through in electronic processing.

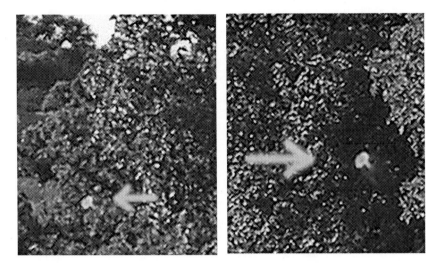

The above shown bright blue, moving orb of light was seen and photographed by Rich while at Enchanted Rock. Could this be an example of the legends of "lights" at this spot? These photos show the object at an interval of about 30 seconds. It appears to have traveled about 50 feet. These photos, and others, can be seen in color at www.paratexas.com.

It wasn't difficult to theorize how the treasure legends could have started, even if there was never any known value to the mining claims. Even before entering the immediate Enchanted Rock area, Mary and I pulled off the road to take a photo about a mile from the great Rock. We found a washout nearby, simply littered with dozens of golf ball sized pieces of white quartz crystal. Almost every piece of rock or boulder had lavish formations of sparkling crystals and flakes, not to mention that the ground everywhere was literally covered with dime and nickel-sized flakes of mica. The effect in the afternoon sun was to give one the impression that the area was indeed enchanted....It was a twinkling wonderland, a geologists dream.

Located only a short 20 to 30 minutes drive from Fredericksburg, the Rock is well into the typical scenic hills. As we followed the winding roads, we crossed photogenic, clear rock bottom streams, and marveled at huge boulders perched at the tops of the small hills.

After parking approximately a quarter mile from the base of the granite dome, we hiked up one of many trails provided for visitors. A large hill next to the dome was composed of huge boulders, punctuated by nooks, crevasses, and caves all along the sides of the impressive structure. At the bottom, a creek flowed in a snake like fashion all along and throughout the trails. Many huge boulders and rock surfaces all along the creek had the appearance of being formed long ago by lava flows. Not being a geologist, neither of us could say for sure, but we had no other explanation for it's smooth, rolling appearance unless it was due to eons of erosion.

Physically, the granite dome certainly lived up to it's name, but we were to quickly discover that the Rock could have been named for it's enchantment from paranormal activity as well.

As usual, Mary and I donned our own digital recording paraphernalia, and headed up the trails keeping a good distance, but well within sight of each other. Little did we know that Enchanted Rock was teeming with ghostly activity....a virtual endless vortex of spiritual voices conversing with each other, and constantly commenting on matters of historical significance, and even matters that seemed to be personal and sounding very much like idle chatter of ordinary people. We heard dozens of spirits speaking their own, or loved ones names.We heard endless references to Indian names and pioneer subjects. Before we would run down our batteries, we would even register comments about our own selves, including the speaking of our names and references to deceased members of our families.

You may remember from a previous mention in this book, that Mary had, so far, encountered mostly a somewhat gentle and proper type of spiritual audience. Although in some cases (as in the Navy ships with ghost sailors), she did catch some teasing and flirting, she has so far been "lucky." We had always stated that we feared someday this tradition would certainly come to an end, as the spirit world does indeed contain some unruly characters. Today, in this intensely active spirit location, a particular ghost expressed his interest in Mary in a rather crude sexual way, and was soon admonished by a friendly spirit who indicated by his protective statement that he was looking out for Mary's interests. After that incident, the unwelcome spirit left and did not come back, much to our relief.

We feel that the previous "warning" from the spirit recorded at the Fredericksburg Jail, was meant to be in reference to this incident. The spiritvoice at the Rock said "do not leave Lieben." And so it was that the guiding spirit and myself as well were to closely accompany Mary on this day....

Normally we are adverse to not reporting the results of our investigations in any way that could cause one to misinterpret the true nature of our findings in the spiritual world. For that reason, we have not omitted the part about the explicit and aggressive language of the spirit that spoke on Mary's tape. But, in this case we must decline to actually provide the exact text of this graphic sequence because the spirit guide who interceded in this incident identified the ghost perpetrator as one inclined to commit illegal and violent offenses. We assume this meant during the perpetrators lifetime, but we were not sure who this was, or what his intentions were. The nature of his rantings was to follow us for approximately three minutes, chanting in cadence with Mary's footsteps. The wording described his selfish desires, in an extraordinarily crude and raucous manner, Oddly, the chanting was almost verse like in construct, and heavily laden with Anglo-Saxon derivative slang.

Immediately after finally losing our unwanted guest, Mary's friendly spirit guide announced "another punk just right above you!"

070- "Another punk just right above you"

This friend from the spirit world had certainly taken a special interest in Mary, and she hopes he will stay around! After that second cautionary message, we had no more unwanted outbursts at the Enchanted Rock. Soon we were constantly receiving input from someone, and often many would be speaking all at once.

The following verse, short but to the point, summed up the spiritual atmosphere at Enchanted Rock for us this day "This place is dead!"

071- "This place is dead !"

That remark was humorous, but at the same time, deadly serious! And with that tone set, we found some of the most unusual EVP we have seen in a long time. The following was a somewhat poetic reflection on contrasting colors, and the contrast between life and death...represented here as a black bird bathed in the white light of love....

072- "Black bird....pretty bird
energy is white.
Black bird....white bird"

This would seem to have been the beginnings of a profound statement of spiritual meaning, but alas, we must have managed to lose contact at the end of the message. No sooner than we had begun to consider the whiteness of light and love, than we were introduced to a random thought of an ordinary citizen of the after death realm, as they simply stated.... "Daddy is broke..." a statement most of us have identified with at sometime, even if we don't know who "Daddy" is....

073- "Daddy is broke..."

A fellow named Fred had friends at the Rock that day. A loved one had this comment.." Fred.....Fred....upset here without you." and then that comment was answered by yet another spirit who complained " Freddy! Talk to him!"

074- "Fred....Fred....upset here without you"

075- "Freddy! Talk to him!"

One of the common considerations that a paranormal investigator has to ponder as in the case of the above EVP, is that the investigator could actually be the one referred to in the message. In this case I momentarily reflected on the possibility that I was in fact "Fred" from a previous life. And in this contact, the ghosts here could have been trying to get my undivided attention. But could they have neglected to note that my name was no longer Fred? You would think not...but then why was I even hearing the message in the first place? If I'm not Fred, then where is he? At this moment, and for most of the time we were at this natural monument, we were isolated from humans except for a rare and occasional passerby.

A couple of personal messages...oddly with the same message but to different names...are these Indian names?

076- "Obelah, forget me"

077- "Pocono, forget me"
And then...one for good ol' Ron....

078- "Ron, keep track of me..."

And here, yet another personal note about Nancy, a cowgirl perhaps? "Pick up the lasso, Nancy"

079- "Pick up the lasso, Nancy"

On this one....I'll let your imagination fill in the blank until you can get a friend with knowledge of dialects in the SE United States, and south of the border....

080-** "That's some HOT P____" **

Fortunately, this was not the creep who came on strong earlier, but there is one or more of these types in every spirit crowd, females as well as males. Some of them just seem to be innocently thinking out loud. Maybe they don't know their private thoughts are being broadcast? Could this be a condition of living in a non material world? Can everyone hear everyone else's thoughts? Whoa...think about that next time you're walking through the mall, alone withn your thoughts, and just admiring the "scenery!?"

Finally, a personal one which I will include....I feel certain this one was meant for me. "Hey...your daddy did not die...ever!"

081- "Hey...your daddy did not die....ever!"

Mary had a very funny message on her recorder, at least it was funny to me. In fact, I tell you, I may actually have made a similar statement myself at some point in my life. Once, years ago when I was very young, my parents moved to Manhattan, Kansas. My Dad had a job at the local school, Kansas State College, and we lived somewhat modestly in this small town environment for less than a couple of years. Strangely enough, the only memories I have of the entire brief time was going to Kansas State with my Dad and sliding down the emergency escape shute from the upper floors, and the museum with the two headed calf. ALL other memories were of the most horrific weather phenomena I've ever known in my life. Walking to school in snow with temps at 15 degrees below zero....Rains and floods that ran us out of two different homes...A hail storm with huge ice balls the size of baseballs that completely ruined our new car, and a huge flood that completely destroyed the entire city and washed out the main bridge to the city downtown. Trips in the car in the countryside found miles and miles of flat boring farm land with nothing to break up the monotony except the weather! Consider my impressions along with the impressions of a very perturbed spirit obviously with a less than favorable life's experience in Kansas.......

082- "Kansas is fucked !...absolutely fucked !...
*   I mean F U C K E D!!"*

And from the "who knows?" department.... "That would be fine"

083- "That would be fine..."

And from the "who cares?" department...."Indian had a house"

084- "Indian had a house"

Almost every EVP session we do has something about a grandpa or grandma in it....the manner of stating this one is suggestive more of days long ago..." hold me, grandpa.....welcome, Godspeed " Was Grandpa receiving a loved one in the afterlife?"

085- "hold me, grandpa.....welcome, Godspeed"

AN ENCOUNTER WITH SPIRICOM?

We had some difficulty filtering the audio of the following messages to standards we like to hold for publishing and presentation to the public. Although they are quite acceptable for interpretation in our lab, they may have small inconsistencies by the time they had been replicated for production for this book. However, we felt that by now you have begun to develop your ear to the subleties of EVP, and we should present these particular EVP samples because of the possibility they may relate to a specific milestone in the study of Electronics Voice Phenomena. An explanation follows;

All who study EVP long for the day we can transmit and receive voice communication to and from the afterlife with instantaneous results and with quality audio control. The truth is, it has been done several times already, but unbelievably, this knowledge has been ignored, repressed, or bypassed for the supposed purpose of keeping mankind on track with their prescribed path in accordance with directives laid out by politics and the worlds controlling societal organizations.

George Meeks founded the Metascience Foundation and sponsored research trips around the world with teams of scientists, researchers and doctors to explore phenomena outside the mainstream of science. In 1980, George worked with a gifted psychic named Bill O'Neil to develop Spiricom, an electrical device that allowed two way communication between the Spirit World and Earth in real time.

Between 1979 and 1982, Spiricom was responsible for generating conditions for transmission of two way conversations between O'Neal and Doc Mueller, a former NASA engineer who passed on in 1967. Dialogue included personal information which was used to verify the contact, and subsequently was adopted as a convincing model for many EVP experimenters.

George Meeks wife passed on in 1990, and during 1991 and 1992, George documented several meaningful contacts with his wife by different electronics means other than just EVP and classified under the term ITC (Instrumental Trans Communication, which includes video, television, telephone, computers, and all other forms of devices which may be capable of communication with the spirit world.)

Konstantin Raudive, an important early pioneer of EVP and ITC, (see chapter on EVP history) collaborated with George Meek's wife from the afterlife, and Raudive proceeded to communicate in several ways with George, as well as other ITC researchers in the US. Sarah Estep, author and president of AAEVP, (American

Association of Electronic Voice Phenomena), Dr Walter Uphoff (president of New Frontiers Center), Hans Heckmann (a close friend and colleague of George Meek) and Mark Macy, author and researcher, all were contacted personally by Konstantine Raudive by 1994. Mark Macy operates a website at this time (worldITC.org), and is current with international studies on ITC and EVP.

The language and dialogue from the following EVP messages recorded at Enchanted Rock, are consistent and in context with the notion that experiments may be desired not only by researcher and experimenters such as myself, but by members of the spirit world as well.

message no. 1, received on Rich's recorder

086- "hear that, Frank? ....It's the radio !....(expletive)....it's the radio Frank !!....SPIRICOM .. back and forth !!"

message no. 2, received on Mary's recorder

087- "Need you to test for me....trust me!"

Our existence on this earth is dwarfed by the reality of the universe and its multi dimensional character.

Embrace the afterlife, do not fear it....it is only you and I, and others like us, all returning to be closer to the oneness of God..........

Rich

Don't Mess With Texas

"Headin' for the house.."

After completing our many adventures in the "haunted" areas of Fredericksburg, we pointed the nose of our Toyota back towards the Houston/Galveston area. We were hot (temps were in low 100's), tired, and the air conditioning blast in the interior of the car was feeling good as we sailed on down the highway. Only about a four hour drive ahead of us, and we would be back in our familiar and comfy home.

After clearing the traffic of the Austin freeways (the halfway point), we headed along a nice straightaway of Hwy 71 towards Columbus where we would join I-10 and roll right on into Houston. Setting my cruise control on 72 mph (speed limit 70 mph,) I cranked up some music, and reflected on the previous days ghostly experiences.

"Ahh, life is good," I mused, as I watched the scenery.

A road sign with the message "Don't Mess With Texas" zipped by my side window, and that TV image of the Indian with a tear in his eye came to mind. This slogan, originally designed to promote a "cleaner, litter free" Texas was, and still is, a popular saying. Now seen on posters and tee shirts everywhere, that popular slogan has, however, been adapted to fit other scenarios.

Like, for instance.....a tall, broad shouldered, Texas State Trooper with a wide brimmed hat in my rear view mirror....lights blazing, and riding on my rear bumper like I was throwing money out the window or something.

"What the hell...?" I said.

"What the hell...?" Mary chimed in.

Since my car was on cruise control, I was finding it hard to believe I was being pulled over for speeding. Suddenly, the trooper fell back into the other lane and pulled up beside the vehicle behind me, gesturing for him to pull over.

Whew...close call, I thought, as Mary and I looked at each other with a basic sigh of relief. I stepped back on the gas and continued on.

In a flash, the trooper was on my rear once more, pulling me over as well as the other car. Two at once. Wow, I thought, what an ambitious cop. He isn't satisfied with only one car, especially when at least one of them (me) wasn't speeding.

Having completed his complicated maneuver of nabbing two criminals at once, Trooper Rambo strolled up towards my vehicle first. With his best imitation of Dirty Harry, and through a stone face grimmace and clenched teeth, he drawled... "May I see your license and insurance papers, sir?"

I handed him my documents, and asked him what the problem was.

"Speeding 78 in a 70 zone, sir"

"MY ASS!" blurted Mary from her passenger side front seat.

"Shhh!, I frantically admonished her out of the side of my mouth. "You want me to go to jail or something ?"

My face surely must have shown genuine astonishment, as I turned back to the officer and muttered..." but..., but..., I had my car on cruise control!"

Trooper Rambo looked at me, and stated, "you weren't going as fast as the other one, I'll just give you a warning ticket."

And with that brief but final declaration, he turned and strolled back to the other car to give them his Dirty Harry impression. If he had three arms, he would have been patting himself on the back at this point with at least one of them.

Finally, the ordeal was finished, we had our prized warning ticket, and we were back on the road with the cruise control set at 67 mph in a 70 mph zone. Mary muttered obscenities under her breath for 10 more minutes, and we conjured up a plan to see if she could get the "Whispering Cowboy" ghost from Alta Loma Cemetery to give a visit to Trooper Rambo. But eventually we abandoned discussing that plan in favor of Mary and our daughter counting the huge traffic in motorcycles on the highway that day who were all on their way to a big biker getogether in the Texas Hill country that week end.

1, 278 motorcycles later, we pulled into our familiar drive, more than ready for some R&R while planning our next ghostly encounter.

And, once again, "Life was Good."

About The Author

It's hard to pin down Rich on his background, but if you take all the parts and pieces you can pry from him one at a time and put them together, it reads something like an adult adventures of Tom Sawyer.

Volunteering for service with the Navy during the Viet Nam war, Rich was sent to lengthy Naval Aviation Electronics Schools, and subsequently attached to a prestigious secret Naval Intelligence spyplane squadron. After reaching his assigned duty station, he attended more schools on flight physiology training, electronics warfare, and received his aircrewman wings as an electronics intelligence equipment operator. He served with two Naval squadrons, and three aircraft carriers, logging flight hours on carriers on the Navy EA3B Skywarrior, as well as lengthy picket flights on the Navy EC121M, a larger aircraft, accumulating well over 100 missions total.

After his Navy tours, his technical electronics schooling had prepared him to work in industrial electronics.....for a brief time in Indianapolis, and then in Houston. But, apparently, this was not suitable to his restless nature. During the late 60's and early 70's, he formed two bands, "Stone Soul Expedition", and "Smithsonian Institute" and successfully entertained on the Indianapolis night club circuit for several years. Later, in the mid seventies, he moved his family to Houston, Texas, started his own custom aquarium specialty display company catering to offshore oil companies, and never looked away from the world of "self employment" again.

As he developed the custom aquarium business in the Houston-Galveston area, he also established contracts with businesses in San Antonio and Austin, including installing and servicing aquarium displays with a state wide restaurant chain. Over the years, he has also worked in political campaign telephone operations, the pet store business, lawn and garden store business, bought and sold properties and kept many for rentals, obtained his private pilots license (owning his own plane), became a certified scuba diver, and started Paranormal Investigations of Texas....and those are just the ones he will talk about.

Rich's technician background provided the groundwork for his excelling in the study of EVP (Electronics Voice Phenomena) which, as a phenomenon little known to the public, captured his interest and has become the basis for some notoriety gained from his internet website WWW.PARATEXAS.COM. Rich's magazine-like website has combined many areas of the paranormal, providing stylized photo spreads with relative editorial content, and accompanied by actual recordings of unknown voices from beyond the confines of our physical reality. (These spirit voices do more than just speak random words...They actually answer questions and give comments on specific subjects!)

Rich seldom does interviews, and the evasiveness adds to the interest in the elusive man. "I'm too busy doin' my own interviews" quips Rich, who is known to be wearing a hidden "wire" recording device most of the time. He has been spotlighted for his ghostly voice recordings acquired from unusual places and events, such as the NASA space center "Columbia On My Mind", and interviews with street people in "Spirits in the Hood."

Rich has a daughter and two grandchildren in Indiana, and Rich and Mary have three children in Texas.

Mary is his "chief motivations officer" as he refers to her admiringly. "Her interest in the paranormal is insatiable, and she is my best partner in investigations." He reflects on their relationship; "She's the most agreeable woman I've ever known, and best of all, she puts up with with ME !"

NOTE: Before playing your CD

It is important that the listener use only a good, CD music quality sound system, or a computer, when listening to the EVP selections on your disk. A quiet, studious atmosphere is strongly recommended, and the use of good quality headsets may be a plus. Turn up the volume, as many of the ghost voices are whispers.

Some of these samples have been engineered to a very narrow frequency range, and if an inferior computer sound card is used or a small or inferior speaker system, the entire voice signal may not be reproduced properly, or an entirely different frequency range signal may partially appear.

Be sure to learn how to set your CD player to "repeat" the EVP selection at least three or more times for each voice sample. It may be necessary with some systems to manually push the return or back button with each repeat. If you are using Windows Media Player on your PC, it has a "repeat" setting on the top bar under "play."

Remember, EVP listening is an acquired ability. Your ear will get better at hearing and translating as you work more and more with EVP. In fact, a large percentage of those who study EVP have reported an increase in development of clairaudient abilities. You'll get back out of it what you put into it!